The Art and Science Connection

Hands-On Activities for Primary Students

Kimberley Tolley

Addison-Wesley Publishing Company

Menlo Park, California • Reading, Massachusetts • New York
Don Mills, Ontario • Wokingham, England • Amsterdam • Bonn
Sydney • Singapore • Tokyo • Madrid • San Juan • Paris
Seoul, Korea • Milan • Mexico City • Taipei, Taiwan

For Bruce

Acknowledgments

I am indebted to the many students and friends who urged me to write this book, but especially to the student teachers and alumni of St. Mary's School of Education, who field-tested these lessons and activities. I would like to thank Mike Kane, managing editor of the Innovative Division of Addison-Wesley, for his interest in this project when it was no more than an idea. For teaching me about various fonts and formats, I would like to thank Anne Janzer. Above all, I am grateful for my patient and helpful husband, Bruce, whose encouragement enabled me to take the initiative and begin to write.

This book is published by Addison-Wesley's Alternative Publishing Group.

Managing Editor: Michael Kane
Project Editor: Priscilla Cox Samii
Production Manager: Janet Yearian
Production Coordinator: Leanne Collins
Design Manager: Jeff Kelly
Text and Cover Design: Christy Butterfield
Illustrations and Cover Art: Kimberley Tolley

ISBN 0-201-45544-7
2 3 4 5 6 7 8 9-ML-96 95 94 93

Contents

Energy *92*

The Theme of Energy 93

Activity Sheet Blackline Masters *125*

Appendix *149*

Preface

What is the connection between art and science? Most people think of the artist and the scientist as living in completely separate worlds. The artist is often thought of as creative, intuitive, and somewhat disorganized, while the scientist is viewed as methodical, orderly, and somewhat calculating. Actually, many scientists bring artistry and creativity to their work, and many artists bring method and order to theirs.

Both scientists and artists have a great curiosity about the world around them. The scientist asks questions about the working of the natural world. The artist asks questions about the ways in which the world can be interpreted and re-created. In seeking answers, the artist uses the processes of perception, creation, and evaluation. The scientist uses the processes of observing, communicating, comparing, ordering, categorizing, relating, and inferring.

Art and science are two different ways of understanding and knowing the world around us. In some instances, the means of arriving at understanding are remarkably similar. Both the artist and the scientist are careful observers of natural phenomena. Both make comparisons of different forms, structures, and interactions, and both communicate and evaluate their findings. The scientist communicates through speaking and writing; the artist communicates through painting, drawing, sculpture, and other art media.

Meaningful art experiences help students develop skills related to creativity and problem solving. In our classrooms, we appreciate that speaking and writing are art forms that are studied in the works of great literature. The visual arts also have a language through which the artist speaks. Students must be given opportunities to understand this language and to learn to analyze what is communicated.

Through science, students can become captivated by the possibilities for discoveries in the natural world. The American poet Walt Whitman characterized science as a limitless voyage of joyous exploration. Exposure to hands-on science investigations provides students with opportunities to develop problem-solving and communication skills.

When students engage in activities that integrate art and science, they learn a variety of ways through which they can understand the world. They learn to bring creativity and insight to the discipline of science, and method and order to the discipline of art. Through the connection of art and science, students increase their appreciation of the natural world and develop an openness to the wonder and joy of life.

Introduction

The Art and Science Connection is a resource for the classroom teacher or specialist interested in integrating art and science. The lessons contained here have been field-tested by teachers in California with students in regular, special education, and ESL (English as a Second Language) classrooms.

The purpose of this curriculum is to provide students with a holistic, hands-on approach to perceiving and learning about the natural world. The lessons simultaneously engage students in the science processes of observing, communicating, comparing, ordering, categorizing, relating and inferring, and in the arts processes of perceiving, creating, and evaluating.

Themes of Science

The American Association for the Advancement of Science (AAAS) has recommended a major emphasis on themes in science curricula. Thematic instruction reinforces the importance of understanding large, overarching concepts rather than the memorization of isolated facts.

The investigations in these lessons are organized around three conceptual themes: *structure, interactions,* and *energy.* These themes are the overarching ideas that integrate the concepts of different scientific disciplines, such as life science, earth science, and physical science. They also integrate the elements and principles of the visual arts and connect the concepts of science and art in meaningful ways.

Lesson Components

A typical lesson contains the following components:

Overview A brief statement of the major focus, or theme, of the lesson.

Student Objectives A listing of the learning and behavioral objectives embedded in the lesson.

Materials A list of materials and resources needed for the lesson.

Getting Ready Step-by-step instructions for setting up demonstration and work areas.

Observing, Comparing, and Describing Guidelines for a discussion in which students share their previous knowledge about the concept(s) to be learned. The opening discussion is usually followed by opportunities for observing, comparing, and describing such natural phenomena as earthworms, ice cubes, or rocks. In some lessons, observing is part of the creative process, as students draw, paint, or sculpt from observation.

Drawing Conclusions
Suggestions for guiding students to share their observations and conclusions and to compare them with concepts they may have held previously. Occasionally this section includes additional information that may be provided by the teacher if appropriate.

Creating
Guidelines for a discussion and demonstration of media techniques introduced in the lesson, as well as suggestions to stimulate creative thinking. In this section of the lesson, students synthesize what they have learned about natural phenomena by creating a work of art.

Evaluating
Suggestions for guiding students to look critically at their own artwork. This is always a positive process. When evaluation consists of a whole-class discussion, input from individual students is voluntary.

Going Further
Suggestions for additional activities or sessions that extend the concepts introduced in the lesson or that connect the lesson with other areas of the curriculum.

Additional Resources
A list of resources useful in extending the lesson or in providing additional background information.

Background Information
Some lessons include this section, which provides additional information about the concepts learned.

Teaching the Lessons

Using the Lesson Format
The lessons contained in *The Art and Science Connection* are written in an organized, step-by-step format. No two classrooms are alike, however, in their interaction with the lesson content. Once a lesson has begun, students may ask questions or need more time on a particular activity. For this reason, the lesson format can only generalize what might occur in the lesson.

Time Frames
Since each classroom is unique, teachers will need to adapt the lessons to the needs of their own students. For some, a particular lesson might take 30 minutes, while for others the lesson is best divided into two sessions of 40 minutes each.

Using Cooperative Learning Strategies
Virtually all of the lessons in *The Art and Science Connection* involve students in activities requiring some form of cooperative group work. If your students have had little experience with cooperative learning, you might wish to begin by having them work with a partner before moving to groups of three or four.

Introduce the idea of cooperative learning by having students talk about how they can help each other and cooperate on projects. Discuss the roles each individual will play in his or her group or pair. Provide modeling and practice so that students understand what cooperative learning looks and sounds like. Finally, after each cooperative learning lesson hold a short debriefing session to allow students to share ways in which they and their partners cooperated well.

An excellent resource for cooperative learning is Elizabeth G. Cohen's book *Designing Groupwork Strategies for the Heterogeneous Classroom,* published by Teachers College Press in New York, 1986.

Management and Planning

Tips for classroom management can be found on page 150 and include suggestions for effective planning, organization, and cleanup. This section is followed by sample letters to parents or guardians requesting donations of materials and supplies.

Structure

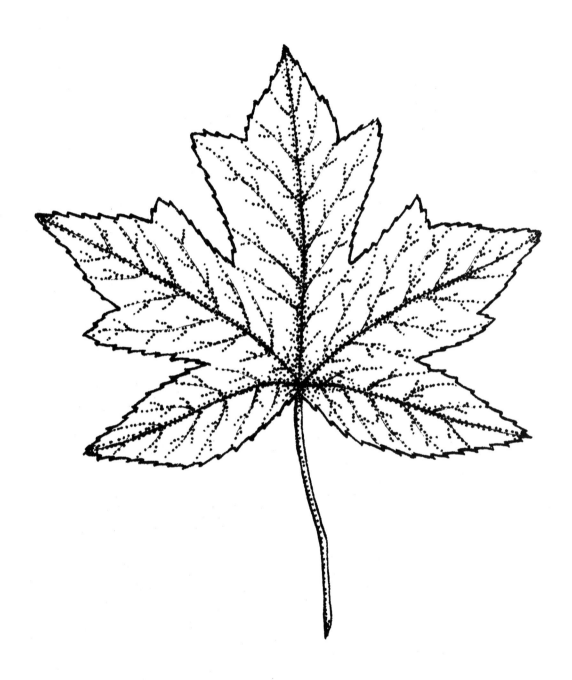

The Theme of Structure

The investigations in this section are organized around the theme of structure. In science, *structure* is defined as "the arrangement of particles or parts in a substance or body." Many kinds of structures are found in the natural world. A leaf, a planet, and an ice crystal each have a structure that can be observed and described. By investigating a variety of biological, physical, and geological forms, students discover how different structures are related.

Structure at different levels of scale reveals different properties at each level. For instance, when first observing a leaf, students might notice its color, shape, stem, and veins. Observing a section of leaf under a microscope reveals an array of plant cells, each with its own microstructure. At another level, students might investigate a leaf as a part of the structure of a tree, which in turn forms part of the structure of a forest habitat.

Structure is an important theme in the visual arts, where it is defined as "a design or organization of independent parts to form a coordinated whole." This organization is achieved through the use of such visual elements as line, color, shape, and space, and such design principles as balance, symmetry, contrast, and repetition. The elements and principles of design contribute to the underlying structure of a work of art. When students are encouraged to notice the elements and principles of design in a painting, drawing, or sculpture, they learn to develop their aesthetic perception through awareness of structure.

Introduction To Structure: The "Ten Questions" Game

Overview

The "Ten Questions" game introduces students to the concept of structure. By playing the game, students learn to describe the structure of any substance through discussion of its properties, such as size, weight, color, shape, and texture. Second- and third-grade students extend their powers of observation and description by proceeding to play "Describe It!," a more advanced version of the game.

Student Objectives

- understand that all matter has properties that can be observed, defined, and recorded.

- observe, compare, and describe the structure of various objects.

Materials

- large brown paper bag

- 2 toys for students to describe

- a collection of 5–10 pairs of objects for students to describe, which might include: 2 rocks, leaves, twigs, shells, books, pencils, erasers, shoes, cups, hats, odd kitchen utensils, and so on

Observing, Comparing, and Describing

note
These activities work especially well when students are able to sit in a circle either on the floor or in chairs.

1. Ask students to name their favorite toy. Say, "How could you describe, or tell about, your toy so that someone else would have a really clear picture of it?"

2. Help students think of words to describe properties, such as: size, weight, color, hardness, shape, texture.

3. Tell students that everything in our world has a structure that can be carefully observed and described. Write the word *structure* on the chalkboard.

4. Hold up a toy, and ask students to notice its parts, such as the arms, feet, head, and trunk of a doll, or the wheels, hood, and bumper of a car. Have students list these parts. Explain that the parts of an object form its structure.

5. Pass the toy around the room, and ask students to think of ways to describe its texture. Explain that *texture* is the way something feels, whether it is rough, smooth, prickly, silky, hard, soft, furry, and so on. To help young students grasp the concept of texture, ask them to make a comparison between the toy and some other object by completing the following sentence: "The toy feels like..." Point out that different parts of the toy may have different textures. Encourage the group to come up with as many comparisons as possible.

6. Pass the second toy around, and ask students to describe another property, such as weight ("It's as heavy as..."), size ("It's as big as..."), and so on.

Playing the "Ten Questions" Game

1. Show students the brown paper bag, and tell them that you are going to place one of the toys in the bag and hide the other. Their job will be to guess which toy is in the bag.

2. Explain the rules:

Guesses must be stated in the form of questions.

The teacher may answer only yes or no to each question.

Students may not ask the name of the object. For instance, they may not ask, "Is it a truck?"

Questions should be about the object's size, weight, color, shape, or texture. For instance, students may ask, "Is it red?" or "Is it as big as a loaf of bread?"

Students who think they know what is hidden in the bag should keep their guesses to themselves until all 10 questions have been asked.

After the group has asked 10 questions, the toy will be removed from the bag and displayed for everyone to see.

3. Model how to ask questions. For instance, you might point to your shirt, and say, "If I were going to hide this shirt in the bag, I might ask: Is it soft? Is it as heavy as a shoe? Does it have stripes? One question I would *not* ask is whether it is a shirt." Allow time for students to practice asking suitable questions.

4. Out of sight of students, place one toy in the paper bag and hide the other. Play the game until all 10 questions have been asked, and then allow students to share their guesses.

5. Tell students they will play the game again with two new objects. Pass the objects around, and have students observe them carefully to notice their size, weight, color, shape, and texture. Then hide one of the objects and place the other one in the bag, and repeat the game. Continue playing as long as it seems appropriate.

note to kindergarten teachers
Because kindergarten students often need more experience observing and describing, you might want to end the first lesson here with a brief review of structure. Many teachers have used different objects and repeated this activity daily for short 10–15-minute sessions until their students are ready to play the "Ten Questions" game.

Drawing Conclusions

Draw students together for a discussion of what they have learned. The following questions are useful in guiding discussion:

What are some different ways to describe something? (*Texture, size, weight, etc.*)

What sorts of questions helped you figure out what was hidden in the bag? (*Questions about the object's properties*)

What do we mean when we talk about structure? (*The parts of an object*)

Playing "Describe It!"

1. To play the game, you will need 5–10 pairs of objects that are very similar, such as two twigs, two rocks, two books, and two plants.

2. Explain the rules:

Students play with a partner. Partners sit face to face; one faces the teacher, and the other sits with his or her back to the teacher. The student facing the teacher is the speaker, and the student with the back to the teacher is the listener.

When partners are in position, the teacher holds up an object for the speakers to observe in silence for several minutes.

When the teacher says, "Describe it!," speakers can begin to talk to their partners. Without saying what the object is, speakers must describe it as carefully as they can to the listeners. Listeners cannot ask questions.

After several minutes, the teacher says, "Stop!" Listeners turn to face the teacher. The teacher holds up two objects for them to see—the object the speakers were describing and a very similar object.

The listeners guess, based on the descriptions given by their partners, which of the two objects the speakers were describing. Students hold up one finger if they guess the first object, and two fingers if they guess the second.

3. When students understand the rules, play the game. After you have revealed the correct object, ask the listeners, "What did your partner say about this object that helped you guess correctly?" When students have had enough time to share, have speakers and listeners switch roles and positions and play the game again with another pair of similar objects.

note

"Describe It!" is a game for second- and third-grade students who have had some experience observing and describing objects. By playing the game, students learn to discriminate between similar objects and describe the structure of an object in detail.

Going Further

Bring art prints or slides to class. Help students observe and describe the structure of paintings, drawings, and sculptures. The following questions are useful in guiding students' perception:

What kinds of lines do you see?

What kinds of shapes do you see?

What colors has the artist used?

How would you describe the texture of this artwork?

Can you find any repetition of line, shape, or color?

Additional Resources

Alexander, Kay. "Developing Aesthetic Perception," in *Learning to Look and Create: The Spectra Program*. Palo Alto, Calif.: Dale Seymour, 1987.

Investigating and Creating with Liquids

Overview

This lesson begins with a game in which the teacher classifies liquids according to a secret rule. After learning that liquids have characteristics by which they can be described, students use the properties of water to create free-flowing designs with tempera paint.

Student Objectives

- observe, compare, classify, and describe liquids.

- become familiar with the various properties of different liquids.

- create abstract designs by blowing tempera paint across paper.

Materials

- (optional) letter to parents or guardians requesting donations, p. 151 (top)

- 5–10 jars with watertight lids, such as small juice bottles or baby food jars, containing liquids of various colors and thicknesses, such as salad oil, shampoo, liquid starch, corn syrup, water, molasses, and dishwashing liquid

- 5–10 solid objects, ranging from hard to soft, such as a pencil, pillow, ball of clay, rock, and marshmallow

- several empty jars of various sizes and shapes

- marker

- 3 containers of liquid tempera paint for each group of two students, with a different color in each container. Add water until the consistency of the tempera is like food coloring or ink.

- plastic teaspoons, 1 per container of tempera paint

- drinking straw per student

- sheet of white construction paper per student

- newspapers to cover desks or tables

- clear jar of liquid tempera paint

Getting Ready

1. Have your students begin collecting clean bottles and jars before you start this lesson. A sample letter to parents or guardians, requesting donations, is included on page 151 (top).

2. Fill the jars with the liquids you have gathered, and place them on a table in front of the classroom, interspersed with the collection of solid objects and empty jars.

3. Use a marker to write the word "IN" in large letters on a sheet of construction paper. Fold the paper so that the IN sign will stand up. Make a similar sign that says "OUT". Place the signs on the table with the liquids and the solid objects, one at either end.

4. Prepare the containers of tempera paint. Place a plastic teaspoon in each container. Arrange the containers, straws, and white paper for easy distribution to students.

5. Have students clear their desks and cover them with newspapers before the lesson.

6. Set aside a place in the classroom where finished paintings can be laid flat to dry.

Observing, Comparing, and Describing

1. Tell students that they are going to play a guessing game. You will be thinking of a special family of objects, and their job will be to guess the name of your family.

2. Take a jar of liquid, place it by the IN sign, and say, "This is *in* my family." Take a solid object, place it by the OUT sign, and say, "This is *out* of my family." Continue placing liquids by the IN sign and solids by the OUT sign until you sense that most students understand your classification scheme.

3. Ask students whether they can guess the name of your family. Sometimes a student will answer, "Your family is things in jars." If this happens, ask the class what name they could give the contents of the jars.

4. Write the word *liquid* on the chalkboard, and tell students that a *liquid* is something that flows. Help students understand that the contents of the jars are liquids.

5. Ask students to tell you their favorite drinks. Point out that the things we drink are liquids. Have students think of other liquids they might encounter around the home, and allow time for sharing.

6. Explain that the structure of a liquid causes it to behave in ways that are very different from something that is solid. Pour one of the liquids into an empty container, and have students notice that the liquid has assumed the shape of the new container. Point out that it would be more difficult to change the shape of a solid.

7. Tell students that they will play the guessing game again in order to learn more about liquids.

8. Repeat the game several times. You might choose clear or colorless liquids to be "in your family." Select such attributes as clearness, thickness, or color of liquids when choosing the rule for classifying into two groups.

9. Conclude the activity by asking, "What is the same about all the things in these bottles?" (*They are all liquids.*) "What are some of the ways they are different?" (*They differ by color, clearness, thickness.*) If necessary, remind students that all the bottles contain liquids by showing how the contents flow.

Creating

1. Tell students that they will be using liquid tempera paint to make wonderful designs. Show students the jar of liquid tempera, and ask them what they notice about its structure. (*It flows, is opaque, colored, etc.*)

2. Explain that in addition to flowing when it is poured, a liquid can flow across a surface such as paper.

3. Demonstrate the procedure:

Use a teaspoon to place a small puddle of tempera paint on the paper.

Use a straw to blow the paint across the surface. Blow the paint as far as you can without going off the paper.

Rotate the paper to change the direction of the paint as you blow.

Repeat the procedure with different colors. Experiment with blowing colors across each other. Continue until the paper is covered with a web of color.

4. Distribute materials. As students create their designs, encourage them to fill the page as completely as they can before beginning a design on a separate sheet of paper.

note
Let students know that they may become short of breath if they blow very hard. Tell them to rest for a while if they begin to feel dizzy.

Drawing Conclusions

When students have finished their designs and have cleaned up their work areas, bring them together for a discussion about what they have learned. The following questions are useful in guiding discussion:

What are liquids? (*Substances that flow*)

Are all liquids the same? (*No*)

What distinguishes them from solids? (*Solids do not flow.*)

How can we use liquids to create paintings? (*We can spread them on paper.*)

Evaluating

Ask students to look at their finished paintings. Have them think of one thing they like about their design and one thing they might do differently next time. Allow time for sharing.

Going Further

- Kindergarten and first-grade students might benefit from extra experience classifying liquids. Fill 15–20 small jars or bottles with a wide variety of liquids, and arrange them in a sturdy box. Students can practice classifying them according to different properties or ordering them serially (for example, from light to dark, or thick to thin). Many teachers have set up a station in the room so that students can explore the liquids independently. Students may record their observations in a journal or logbook.

- Have your students make lists of "safe" and "poisonous" liquids as part of a safety lesson.

- Extend the art activity with older students by having them create a collage with pieces of paper torn from their straw-blown designs. The torn papers may be mounted in the collage with contrasting pieces of paper in solid colors.

Additional Resources

Agler, Leigh. *Liquid Explorations*. Berkeley, Calif.: Lawrence Hall of Science, University of California, 1987.

Elementary Science Study: Drops, Streams, and Containers. Hudson, N.H.: Delta Education, 1986.

Investigating and Creating with Solids

Overview

What is a solid? After observing and comparing different solids, students predict which materials will break apart, bend, or stick to paper. They observe that when such solids as graphite pencil, chalk, and wax crayon are rubbed against paper, they leave small particles behind. Finally, students use the properties of solids by creating a mixed-media drawing with art chalk and wax crayon.

Student Objectives

- observe that a solid tends to keep its shape when it is left alone.

- observe that not all solids have the same structure. Some are stronger and more flexible than others.

- use two solid materials—chalk and wax crayon—in creating a mixed-media drawing.

Materials

- large sheet of white butcher paper, and masking tape

- a collection of solid objects, ranging from hard to soft, such as a rock, ball of modeling clay, stick of chalk, a crayon, sponge, cushion, dried leaf, piece of bread, and baseball bat

- rubber eraser

- pencil

- newspaper to cover work areas

- white drawing paper, 1 per student plus 1 for the teacher

- facial tissues, 1 per student plus 1 for the teacher

- art chalk in assorted colors

- wax crayons in dark colors, such as black, dark blue, green, purple, and red

- old rags or towels

- water

- (optional) Activity Sheet 1: Solids in My Home (page 126)

Getting Ready

1. Tape the butcher paper to the front wall or chalkboard.

2. Set the collection of solid objects, the eraser, and the pencil near the demonstration area.

3. Cover work areas with newspaper.

4. Arrange the drawing paper, facial tissues, art chalk, and crayons for easy distribution during the lesson.

5. Soak old cloths in water and wring out until damp. Students can use these to wipe their hands clean during cleanup. (See "Tips for Working with Art Materials" on page 152.)

Observing, Comparing, and Describing

1. Ask students whether they have ever heard someone say, "rock solid" or "frozen solid." Ask what they think these expressions mean.

2. Show students the collection of solid objects. Tell them that a *solid* is something that keeps its shape when it is left alone. Write the word *solid* on the chalkboard.

3. Explain that not all solids have the same structure; they can be very different. Some solids are hard, some are soft, some are smooth, and so on. Ask students to tell you how the solids in your collection are different. Help them talk about differences in weight, texture, shape, and hardness.

4. Ask students to predict which solids in your collection will bend. As you point to each item, students can signal their prediction with a thumbs-up or thumbs-down.

5. Have one or several volunteers come up and test the group's predictions. Point out that even though some solids can bend, they will keep their shape when they are left alone.

6. Take the pencil, and draw several dark lines across the butcher paper. Explain that the reason the pencil leaves a line is that tiny particles of the graphite break off and stick to the paper.

7. Ask students to predict which solids will leave a line or smudge on the butcher paper. Have volunteers test the group's predictions.

8. Remind students that in order to leave a mark, a solid must break and then stick to the paper.

9. Have students notice the solids that left marks on paper. Ask them to predict which of these solids will stick best to the paper. Point out that a solid that sticks well will be hard to erase. Have volunteers test the group's predictions by attempting to erase the marks on the butcher paper.

Drawing Conclusions

1. Have students discuss what they have learned. Questions to guide discussion include the following:

What is a solid? (*A substance that keeps its shape when left alone*)

How do solids differ? (*Color, texture, hardness, etc.*)

2. Tell students that artists make use of solids that break and stick to paper. Examples include pencils, crayons, and chalk. Tell students that next they will make drawings that use two solids: chalk and crayon.

3. Ask students to talk about the differences in the way the crayon and chalk stick to paper. Explain that as they draw, they will be able to feel and see these differences.

Creating

1. Explain that the first step is to use the art chalk to color every inch of the paper. Demonstrate how to hold a piece of chalk on its side and rub it back and forth over an area of the paper that is roughly the size of your hand.

2. Next, take another color and rub an area next to the first. Continue using different pieces of chalk until the entire paper is covered with different patches of color.

3. Take a facial tissue and show students how to rub the chalk surface to blend the edges of the colored areas together. Move the tissue in a circular motion as you go over the paper.

4. Explain that the chalk can be blended and smudged with the tissue because it does not stick well to the paper's surface. Have students notice the chalk on your fingers, and point out that their hands will become stained as well. Explain that they should not worry, since the chalk will wipe off easily later with a damp cloth.

5. Have students look at the colored chalk background you have made, and ask what it makes them think of. (Perhaps it makes them think of flowers or the sea.)

6. Next, take a black or other dark wax crayon. Explain that you now will draw over the chalk with the wax crayon. Tell students that if the background makes them think of the sea, they might want to draw different kinds of fish swimming. Or, they might draw flowers or houses. Have students share as many ideas as possible at this stage.

7. Using the crayon, draw a picture over the background. Leave spaces between your lines so that the background comes through.

note

Roll up your sleeves before you start, and have your students do the same before they begin to use the chalk. Explain that they should try not to touch their clothes as they work. Remind them that since chalk does not stick very well to things, it will rub off easily on paper, hands, and clothes.

8. Have students review the steps of the drawing process: covering the paper with chalk, blending the edges with tissue, then drawing over the chalk with wax crayon.

9. Distribute materials so that students can begin drawing. Circulate, and offer assistance when necessary.

Evaluating

1. After cleanup, display the finished drawings. Ask students whether they can find examples of blending—where the artist used tissue to smooth the chalk.

2. Ask volunteers to think of one thing they really like about their drawing and to share it with the class.

Going Futher

- Have students use Activity Sheet 1: Solids in My Home to record different kinds of solid objects at home.

- Students will enjoy exploring the properties of modeling clay, which is a very flexible solid. A station can be set up in an area of the room, with construction paper place mats and modeling clay. Students can be encouraged to see how many different shapes they can make with the clay.

- Have students investigate the weight of different solids. Given a collection of solid items, students can predict the weights by ordering the items serially—for example, from heaviest to lightest. Next, students can use a balance scale to test their predictions.

Additional Resources

Lowery, Lawrence F. "Solids," in *The Everyday Science Sourcebook*. Palo Alto, Calif.: Dale Seymour, 1985.

Exploring the Properties of Sand

Overview

Is sand a liquid or a solid? What do its grains look like? Students investigate the properties of sand to discover answers to these questions. Then, using sand, glue, and colored construction paper, they create paintings with linear designs.

Student Objectives

- observe that sand is a solid, made up of tiny particles called grains.

- observe that a sample of sand may contain grains that are very different in structure.

- use sand, glue, and paper to create paintings with linear designs.

Materials

- sand, approximately 1/2 cup per student

- small containers to hold sand, such as paper cups or cut-off milk cartons, 1 per student

- white glue

- small containers to hold glue, 1 per group or student pair

- plastic teaspoons, several per container of glue

- newspaper to cover work areas

- hand lenses, 1 per student pair

- light-green or blue construction paper, 8" x 11", 1 per student pair

- (optional) Activity Sheet 2: Looking at Grains of Sand (page127)

- dark-colored construction paper, 18" x 12", 1 sheet per student plus 1 for the teacher

Getting Ready

1. Pour sand into its containers. Pour glue into its containers. Place several teaspoons into each container of glue.

2. Arrange materials for easy distribution during the lesson.

3. Cover work areas with newspaper.

4. Set aside an area of the room where the sand paintings can dry overnight.

note
Students should be organized into pairs for the lesson.

Observing, Comparing, and Describing

1. Have students watch as you pour some sand from your hand into an empty container. Ask students whether they can guess what you are pouring. If necessary, have volunteers come up, examine the sand, and share their observations with the class.

2. Tell the class that the substance is sand. Have students share what they know about sand. The following questions are useful in guiding discussion:

What is sand? (*A gritty material*)

What is it made of? (*Very small particles of rock*)

Where can you find it? (*Beach, etc.*)

3. Remind students that a *liquid* is something that flows. Pour some sand again as students watch, and ask them whether they think sand is a liquid. Have students notice that the sand is dry, not wet. Help them understand that sand is not a liquid even though it can be poured.

4. Remind students that a *solid* is something that keeps its shape when it is left alone. Pour a little pile of sand onto a piece of newspaper. Ask, "Will this sandpile keep its shape if we leave it alone?" (*Yes*) Help students understand that sand is made up of tiny pieces of solids, called *grains*.

5. Ask students whether they think every grain of sand looks alike. How might grains differ? (*Shape, size, color*)

6. Tell students that you will be giving every pair a hand lens, a sheet of light-blue or green construction paper, and two containers of sand. They then will pour some grains of sand onto the paper and examine them with the hand lens. Demonstrate the procedure.

7. Tell students to find as many different kinds of sand grains as they can. They should look for different colors, shapes, and sizes.

8. Optional: Second- and third-grade students may be given Activity Sheet 2: Examining Grains of Sand on which to record their observations.

9. Distribute the materials. Circulate, and offer assistance as students examine the sand.

Drawing Conclusions

1. Have students share their observations.
The following questions can be used to guide discussion:

How did the size of the grains differ? (*Some were larger than others.*)

What different colors did you find? (*Clear, tan, pink, etc.*)

What shapes did you find? (*Round, square, pointed, or jagged shapes*)

Were some grains shinier than others? (*Yes*)

2. Explain that sand is made up of different kinds of grains.
Each grain was once a part of a kind of rock, each with its
own structure. Some grains are very hard or heavy or shiny.
Others are soft or light or dull.

Creating

1. Tell students the properties of sand make it useful to artists.
Because it can be poured and its small grains will stick to paper
with glue, artists can use sand to create paintings.

2. Demonstrate the procedure. Place a sheet of dark-colored
construction paper on a surface covered with newspaper.

3. Dip a teaspoon into the white glue, and wipe it on the edge of
the container to remove the excess. Hold the teaspoon over the
paper, and slowly pour a thin stream of glue onto the paper.
Move your hand slowly over the paper as you pour so that the
glue creates lines on the surface. Cover the entire surface of the
paper with a web of lines.

4. Gently shake the container of sand over the lines of glue. When
you have poured out all the sand, grasp the sides of the paper
and lift so that the excess sand falls toward the center of the
paper. Tilt the paper over the sand container so that the excess
sand falls back inside.

5. Point out that much of the sand will have fallen on the
newspaper. Show students how to fold the newspaper so that
the sand can be poured back into the container for reuse.

6. Distribute materials so that students can begin working.
Circulate, and offer assistance when needed.

Evaluating

When the paintings are dry, display them in the room. Have
students notice the variety of lines created by their peers. Ask
volunteers to talk about one thing they especially like in their
paintings.

Going Further

- Visit your local library to find picture books on Navajo sand paintings to share with students.

- Older students can make plaster sand sculptures. Mix sand with plaster of Paris. Add water, and pour into empty milk cartons. Let the plaster mold harden completely overnight. Students can carve animal or abstract forms from the sand blocks, using old stainless steel butter knives.

Additional Resources

Sisson, Edith A. "Sandy Shores," in *Nature With Children of All Ages.* New York: Prentice-Hall, 1982.

Exploring the Properties of Rocks in Mosaics

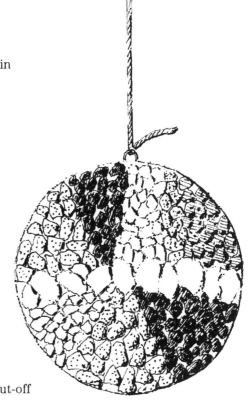

Overview

In this activity, students observe, describe, and classify rocks in order to learn about differences in their structures. They then make use of differences in color, shape, and texture to arrange pebbles into mosaic designs.

Student Objectives

- observe that rocks are of many different kinds, each with its own structure.

- understand that mosaics are made up of small pieces of glass, stone, tile, rock, or other materials.

- create a pebble mosaic plaque.

Materials

- 4 kinds of small rocks and pebbles (see "Getting Ready" below)

- 4–5 brown paper lunch bags

- small containers to hold pebbles, such as paper cups and cut-off milk cartons

- self-lock plastic bags, 1 per group of 3–4 students

- plastic coffee can lids or margarine tub lids, 1 per student (you may substitute small aluminum pie tins)

- newspapers to cover desks

- strip of cloth to use as a blindfold

- (optional) Activity Sheet 3: Classifying Rocks (page 128)

- white glue

- small paper clips

- yarn or string

Getting Ready

1. Obtain rocks from a gardening center that specializes in rocks for landscaping. (Look in the Yellow Pages under "Rock.") Take brown paper lunch bags with you to the center, and fill 4 of them, each with a different kind of rock, 1/4 inch to 1/5 inch in diameter. You should be able to find several colors of granite, pumice (lava rock), dolomite, and other kinds of rock. In addition to bags of small pebbles, gather 30 larger pieces (about 1 inch in diameter) of each type of rock.

2. For each group of students, fill several small containers with pebbles; that is, one with yellow granite, one with dolomite, and so on.

3. For each group of students, fill one self-lock plastic bag with larger rocks, several of each kind.

4. Arrange larger rocks, containers, and lids for easy distribution during the lesson.

5. Cover work areas with newspaper.

6. Set aside an area of the room where the mosaic plaques can dry for several days.

Observing, Comparing, and Describing

1. Ask for a volunteer to come forward. Blindfold the student and tell him or her that you are going to put something in his or her hand, and that his or her job will be to guess what the object is.

2. Show the class a rock, and have the group predict whether the volunteer will be able to guess what it is when he or she touches it. Let the volunteer feel the rock and ask him or her to guess. Then, remove the blindfold so that the volunteer can see the rock.

3. Ask students to share what they know about rocks. The following questions are useful in guiding discussion:

How do rocks feel? (*Hard, smooth, rough, etc.*)

What different colors can rocks be? (*Gray, green, brown, white, pink, etc.*)

How small can a rock be? (*Almost as small as a grain of sand*)

How large can a rock be? (*As big as a huge boulder*)

Where can you find rocks? (*Almost anywhere*)

4. Explain that rocks are of many different kinds, each with its own structure. Remind students that the parts of an object form its *structure* (See Lesson 1.) The parts of a rock that we can describe are its size, weight, color, texture, and shape.

5. Tell students that you are going to give them a problem to solve. Show them a plastic bag filled with different kinds of rocks. Explain that several different kinds of rocks will be in the bag, all mixed up. Their job is to work in groups and to classify, or sort, the rocks.

note

Students should be organized into groups of three or four for this activity.

Modifications for kindergarten are described in the note on the next page.

6. Demonstrate by showing students two rocks that look the same. Tell students that if everyone in their group agrees that these two rocks belong in the same pile, they should be placed together. Show students how to place the rocks together on their desks or table.

7. Optional: second- and third-grade students can use Activity Sheet 3: Classifying Rocks to record their observations.

8. Distribute the rocks, and have students begin classifying them. Circulate, and offer assistance when needed.

Drawing Conclusions

Have students talk about the differences they noticed among the various kinds of rocks. If appropriate, tell students the names of the various kinds, such as granite and dolomite.

Creating

1. Tell students that artists use materials like rocks to create mosaics. Explain that a mosaic is made by placing many small pieces of rock, tile, glass, or other items together to make a pattern or design.

2. Explain that by placing the same kinds of rocks together they can create areas of color in a mosaic.

3. Demonstrate how to make a pebble mosaic plaque. Take a coffee can or margarine tub lid. In one area, set pebbles of one kind. Set the pebbles close together. In another area, set pebbles of a different kind.

4. When students understand the process, distribute the lids and containers of pebbles. Allow them to proceed, and offer assistance when necessary.

5. When students have finished, have them carefully carry their lids to an undisturbed area of the room.

6. Later, squeeze enough white glue into every lid to fill it to the brim. Tilt the end of a small paper clip over the edge of the brim into the glue.

7. After the plaques have dried for several days, pop them out of the plastic molds and hang them up with yarn or string.

note to kindergarten teachers

If your students need more practice with classification before working in groups on this activity, the lesson can be modified as follows:

Have students sit in a circle. Give each child several rocks, one of each kind. Hold up a rock, and ask students to think about which of their rocks is most like yours.

Place your rock on the floor in the middle of the circle. Next, have students take the rock they think is most like yours and place it in a pile with the first.

When everyone has placed a rock in the pile, ask students to talk about how the rocks are the same. Repeat the procedure with each kind of rock.

Evaluating

Display the finished mosaic plaques. Have students notice the different designs made by their peers. Ask them to talk about how they might use other materials to make a similar mosaic.

Going Further

- Students can investigate the weight of different rocks. Set up a station in the room, equipped with a balance scale and collection of rocks. Have students predict the weight of the rocks and then weigh their rocks to find the lightest and heaviest.

- Students can investigate the hardness of different rocks. Give groups of students a stainless steel butter knife, a penny, and a glass jar. Have them order rocks from soft to hard according to (a) whether they will scratch a penny, (b) whether they will scratch steel, or (c) whether they will scratch glass.

- Have students each bring in a large rock, about the size of an apple or grapefruit. Have students use tempera paint and small brushes to paint a picture or design on the top of their rocks. Varnish the completed surfaces, and then let students take their rocks home as doorstops.

Additional Resources

Alexander, Kay. "Bean and Seed Mosaic," in *Learning to Look and Create: The Spectra Program, Grade One*. Palo Alto, Calif.: Dale Seymour, 1987.

Elementary Science Study: Rocks and Charts. Hudson, N.H.: Delta Education, 1986.

Sisson, Edith A. "Activities With Rocks and Soil," in *Nature With Children of All Ages.* New York: Prentice-Hall, 1982.

Exploring the Structure of Earthworms

Overview

Does an earthworm have eyes? Which end is the head? In this activity, students investigate earthworms in order to learn about the animals' external structures. They then apply their knowledge in creating earthworm potato prints.

Student Objectives

- observe, compare, and identify various parts of the external structure of an earthworm.

- use multiple prints to create a shape.

Materials

- 1 earthworm per student

- potatoes, sliced, for printing as described in "Getting Ready"

- 2–3 shallow containers of tempera paint per group of 4 students: black, red, blue, or purple

- *For grades 1–3:* 2 large sheets of white or colored construction paper per student

- paper plates

- 1 hand lens per group of 4 students

- newspaper to cover work areas

- (optional) Activity Sheet 4: Looking at Earthworms (page 129)

- *For kindergarten:* large sheet of butcher paper for each group of 4 students

Getting Ready

1. Obtain earthworms, either from your garden or from a bait shop (see the Yellow Pages for one near you). Keep them refrigerated in a container with some damp earth until ready to use. Feed them cornmeal, coffee grounds, or compost.

2. Slice potatoes as follows: First, slice each potato in half lengthwise. Next, slice the halves crosswise so that each slice is about 1/2 inch wide.

3. Arrange potatoes, tempera paint, and construction paper for easy distribution.

4. Arrange the container of earthworms, paper plates, and hand lenses for easy distribution during the lesson.

5. Cover work areas with newspaper.

note

Students should be arranged in groups of four during the activity.

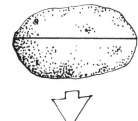

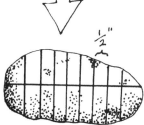

Observing, Comparing, and Describing

1. Ask students to tell you what they know about earthworms. Allow time for sharing.

2. Review the concept of structure with students. Write the word *structure* on the chalkboard, and remind students that the parts of an object form its structure. Explain that today they will be investigating the structure of an earthworm.

3. Explain that an earthworm is a living animal and must be handled gently and with respect. Demonstrate how to lift an earthworm carefully by sliding your fingers under it.

4. Tell students that their earthworms will be on paper plates and should be handled as little as possible.

5. Explain that students will be investigating worms to discover as much as they can about their structure. The following questions encourage careful observation:

Compare your worm with your group members' worms. How are they alike? Different?

How can you tell its head from its rear? Its top from its bottom? (*The head end is pointed and is near the clitellum band. The top is darker than the bottom.*)

Does your worm have eyes? (*No*) A mouth? (*Yes*)

Does your worm have a blood vessel running the length of the worm? (*Yes*) What color is it? (*Purple*)

Is the worm smooth? (*It is segmented. Its top is smooth, but the underside is rough.*)

6. Optional: Older students can use Activity Sheet 4: Looking at Earthworms to guide their observations.

7. Distribute a plate of four worms to each group of four students, along with extra plates and hand lenses. As students investigate, circulate, and offer assistance where needed.

Drawing Conclusions

1. Collect the worms, plates, and hand lenses. Gather students together for a discussion of what they have learned. List observations on the chalkboard.

2. For more information about earthworms, see "Earthworms: Background Information" on page 26.

note

Some students will not want to touch the earthworms at all. These students can be encouraged to work with partners who are willing to handle the worms for them while they observe.

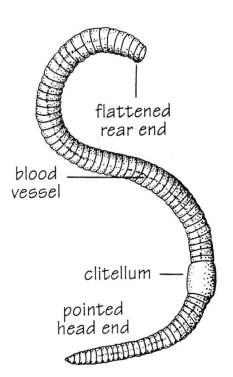

flattened
rear end

blood
vessel

clitellum

pointed
head end

SAFETY TIP

Make sure students wash their hands after handling the worms.

Creating

1. Show students how to hold a potato slice so that the rectangular side can be used for printing.

2. Dip the potato into the tempera, and then wipe excess paint off on the side of the container. Stamp a series of rectangles in a row with their widths touching or slightly overlapping. The result will look like the segments on the body of a worm.

3. Stamp the pointed head end, and use the semicircular side of the potato to stamp the tail end. The clitellum can be made by stamping a slightly wider section of the body.

4. For Kindergarten: Explain that four students will be stamping their worms on the same large sheet of butcher paper. (Kindergartners have difficulty making curves in their worms, so their worms should lie fairly straight across the length of the paper.)

5. For Grades 1–3: Show students how to stamp a curve in the worm's body. Holding one end of the potato stationary, stamp out a fan shape to make a curve. Tell students that they will need to practice several times to get it right.

6. As students work, encourage them to use different colors to create second and third worms on their papers. Explain that worms can cross over each other in an interesting tangle.

Evaluating

Display the finished work. Ask students to look at their prints and to think of one thing they like about them and one thing they might do differently next time. Allow time for sharing.

Going Further

- Have students extend their knowledge of earthworms by providing additional sessions in which they can explore. Have students record their observations in a journal or logbook. The following questions are useful in guiding further investigations:

  How does a worm respond to a puff of air? (*It draws back.*)

  Does it move faster when warm or cold? (Worms can be warmed or cooled by placing them in warm or cool tap water for about 30 seconds.) (*It moves faster when warm.*)

  How does a worm respond to gravity? What happens when it is placed on a tilted surface? (*It travels upward.*)

  Does it seem to prefer wet or dry soil? (*Wet*)

  How does it react to darkness or light? (*It moves toward darkness.*)

- Keep earthworms in a clear plastic or glass container filled loosely with fresh damp soil. Cover the sides with black construction paper for several days. Remove the paper and study the worm tunnels. Can students find any worm egg cases?

Additional Resources

Buchsbaum, Ralph. *Animals Without Backbones*. Chicago: University of Chicago Press, 1987.

Kramer, David C. "Earthworms," in *Animals in the Classroom*. Menlo Park, Calif.: Addison-Wesley, 1989.

• •

Earthworms: Background Information

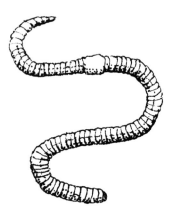

Earthworms contribute to the growth of plants by breaking down the decaying matter in the soil. The air necessary for plant growth enters the soil through worm burrows.

The smooth body of the earthworm is made up of rings, or segments, called *annuli*. On each segment, except the first and the last, are four pairs of tiny bristles. These bristles, called *setae*, help the worms move through the earth.

Earthworms have no eyes or ears, but they do have a mouth. They are sensitive to heat, light, and touch.

Earthworms have no lungs or gills. The worms breathe through their skin, which is in contact with the air found between the small particles of soil. When it rains, these air spaces fill with water, and the worms must come to the surface to breathe, or they die.

Each earthworm has both male and female reproductive parts. Each worm must mate with another to form eggs. Eggs are laid in a cufflike structure provided by the *clitellum*. As the worm moves, the cuff slides along the body and over the head. It then closes completely around the eggs to make a saclike cocoon. After several weeks in the cocoon, the young worms hatch.

Exporing the Structure of Snails

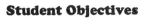

Overview

Do snails have teeth? How do they move? How many spirals are in a snail's shell? In this activity, students investigate snails in order to learn about their external structure. They then apply their knowledge by creating mixed-media drawings of snails, using chalk and tempera paint.

Student Objectives

- observe, compare, and identify various parts of the external structure of snails.

- use chalk and tempera paint to create a mixed-media drawing of a snail.

Materials

- land snails, 1 per student

- pieces of clear plastic, approximately 3" x 4", 1 per group or student pair

- newspaper to cover work areas

- sturdy paper plates, plastic foam trays, or aluminum pie tins, 1 per student

- 1 hand lens per pair or group of students

- honey, 1 dab per student

- lettuce, 1 tiny piece per student

- (optional) Activity Sheet 5: Looking at Snails (page 130)

- (optional) large sheet of butcher paper

- colored art chalk

- assorted colors of liquid tempera paint

- white construction paper, 12" x 18", 1 per student plus 1 for the teacher

- brushes

- shallow containers for paint

Getting Ready

1. Obtain land snails from your yard, or have students bring them from home. Snails are most easily found during fall and spring months. During the day they rest on the underside of leaves or at the base of walls and fences. During the evening or early morning hours, they can be found on lawns. Otherwise, purchase them from a pet shop or a science supply house.

2. Keep snails in a tightly covered, large container with ventilation. Snails are very active at night and will crawl around the classroom if they escape. Sprinkle the snails with water daily. Feed them cornmeal, greens, and bits of eggshell.

3. Obtain 3" x 4" pieces of clear plastic from a discount framing shop, lumber yard, or decorating center.

4. Arrange materials for easy distribution during the lesson.

5. Cover work surfaces with newspaper.

Observing, Comparing, and Describing

1. Ask students to tell you what they know about snails. Allow time for sharing.

2. Ask students what they would like to find out about snails. Provide examples of questions they could ask, such as the following:

Do snails have eyes? (*Yes*)

Do they have teeth? (*They have a teethlike structure.*)

3. Review the concept of *structure* with students. Write the word *structure* on the chalkboard, and remind students that the parts of an object form its structure. Explain that today they will be investigating the structure of snails.

4. Explain that a snail is a living animal and must be handled gently and with respect. Demonstrate how to lift a snail carefully by its shell. Tell students that the snails should be kept on paper plates most of the time.

5. Tell students that they will be investigating the snail to discover as much as they can about its structure. The following questions encourage careful observation:

Compare your snail with your group members' snails. How are they alike? Different?

How many spirals are in your snail's shell? Does every snail have the same number? Does the spiral curve to the left or to the right?

Place your snail on a clear piece of plastic and watch your snail from below. How does its foot move? What does the snail leave behind on the plastic?

note
Students should be organized in pairs or small groups for this lesson.

note
Some students will not want to touch a snail. These students can be encouraged to work with partners who are willing to handle the snails for them while they observe.

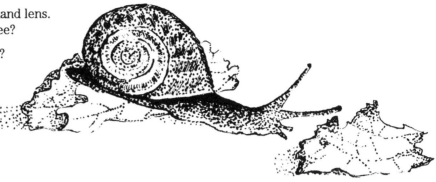

Look closely at your snail with a hand lens.
What colors and designs do you see?

Hold your snail. Is it warm or cool?
Wet or dry? Heavy or light?

Put some honey on your finger,
and present it to your snail.
What does the snail do?
How does it feel? Can
you see the snail's teeth?
How does the tongue move?

Place some lettuce near your snail. Listen to the snail eat the
food. What kind of sounds does it make as it eats?

How many tentacles does a snail have? (Most land snails have
two pairs, while aquatic snails have one pair.) What happens
when you touch one lightly? Can you find the snail's eyes?
(The eyes are at the tips of the longer tentacles.)

For Kindergarten–Grade 1: Select just a few questions for your
students to investigate. Pose the questions, demonstrate how to
investigate, and then have students begin working with the
snails. When students have completed the investigations, pose
several more questions as seems appropriate.

6. Optional: Older students may use Activity Sheet 5: Looking at
Snails to guide their observations.

Drawing Conclusions

1. Collect the snails, and gather students together to share their
observations. You might wish to record these on the chalkboard
or on a sheet of butcher paper.

2. For more information about snails, see "Snails: Background
Information" on page 31.

Creating

1. Tell students that they will be using chalk and tempera paint to
make a drawing of a snail. Explain that a drawing that uses more
than one kind of art material is called a *mixed-media* drawing.

2. Take a large sheet of white construction paper. Demonstrate the
procedure: First, place your hand squarely in the middle of the
paper with your fingers spread apart. Tell students your hand is
a guide. Take a piece of chalk, and draw a large semicircle, or
arc, above your hand.

3. Remove your hand, and connect the ends of the semicircle with
a horizontal line, as shown.

4. Ask students how many spirals their snail has. Show students
how to draw the spirals inside the shell shape.

SAFETY TIP
Make sure students wash their hands after
handling the snails.

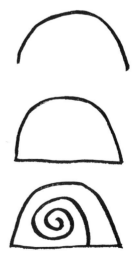

5. Next, draw the snail's foot and head. As you are drawing, point out the tentacles. Remind students that the two upper tentacles contain the eyes and are longer.

6. Using different colors of chalk, draw patterns on the snail's shell. Leave white spaces for the tempera paint.

7. Show students how to take a brush, dip it into the paint, and wipe the excess against the edge of the container. Apply patches and spots of color between the chalk lines. Show students how to take the chalk and draw over the wet tempera to make more lines and designs.

8. Tell students that they may paint the background and body of the snail any color they like. Explain that an artist can be creative and may paint a yellow, red, or blue snail.

9. When students understand the procedure, distribute the materials. Help students draw the shell shape around their hands. Be sure every student has drawn a large shape, one that fills the paper. As students work to complete their snail drawings, circulate, and offer assistance when necessary.

Evaluating

Display the finished work. Have students notice the patterns created by their peers. Allow volunteers to share one thing they especially like about their own drawings.

Going Further

■ Have students extend their knowledge of snails by providing additional sessions in which they can explore. Have students record their observations in a journal or logbook. The following questions are useful in guiding investigation:

How does a snail respond to a puff of air? (*It probably retracts its tentacles or pulls back into its shell.*)

Place a snail on a plastic plate, and tilt the plate. How does the snail respond to gravity? (*Crawls upwards*)

Place a snail on a dry sponge, then on a wet sponge. What happens? (*It probably moves faster on the wet sponge.*)

Can a snail walk a tightrope? Use a length of string to find out. (*Yes*)

How fast can your snail move? Organize a race to see whose snail moves the fastest.

■ Have students write stories about a day in the life of a snail.

Additional Resources

Henwood, Chris. *Snails & Slugs.* New York: Watts, 1988.

Kramer, David C. "Snails," in *Animals in the Classroom.* Menlo Park, Calif.: Addison-Wesley, 1989.

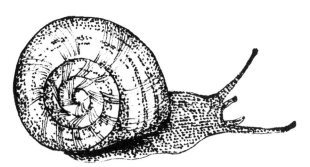

Snails: Background Information

The snail has no internal skeleton. Inside its shell, it has a small, simple brain, a two-chambered heart, a digestive system, a liver, a lung, kidneys, reproductive organs, and a nervous system.

The land snail has eyes in its two upper tentacles, with which it can detect only light and dark. The lower antennae contain organs of smell. The snail breathes through a tiny opening, its lung, which is located on the right side of its body near the rim of the shell. The snail has a long, narrow tongue, the *radula*, which is covered with 27,000 tiny, hooked teeth, arranged in rows. As the snail eats, its tongue moves back and forth like a small saw.

The snail's foot secretes mucus to help the snail move over many different kinds of surfaces. The snail moves only 2 or 3 inches per minute. Its movements are usually uphill or upward toward shadow, moisture, or food.

Snails are *hermaphroditic*, containing both male and female reproductive organs. When snails mate, the feet join together. After mating, the snail lays approximately 30 white eggs in a hole in the soil. The eggs develop in 10 days to 4 weeks, depending on the moisture and warmth of the environment. The shells of baby snails have only one spiral and are formed in the egg.

Exploring the Structure of Fish

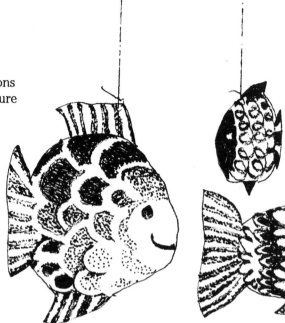

Overview

In this activity, students observe and compare two or more kinds of fish. They draw conclusions about the similarities and differences in structure among various species. They then apply their knowledge by creating fish mobiles to hang in the room.

Student Objectives

- observe that all fish have gills through which they breathe.

- compare the fins, tails, and scales of different species and observe that they may vary in structure.

- use linear patterns in creating designs for fish mobiles.

Materials

- *For grades 2–3:* Activity Sheet 6: Looking at Fish (page 131)

- 1 guppy and 1 goldfish per group of 4 students, *or* pictures of different kinds of fish, several per group

- clear glass containers to hold fish, such as small jars

- liquid tempera paint in assorted colors

- wax crayons

- large sheet of butcher paper and masking tape

- newspaper to cover work areas

- brushes

- containers for paint and for water

- *For kindergarten–grade 1:* Activity Sheet 7: Fish Outline (page 132), 2 per student

- scissors

- *For grades 2–3:* 12" x 18" white construction paper, 2 sheets per student

- facial tissue

- stapler

- hole punch

- string or yarn

Getting Ready

1. If you will be using live fish, obtain guppies and small goldfish from your local pet store, along with a sufficient supply of food and a container or aquarium in which to keep them in the classroom after the investigation. Place one goldfish and one guppy in a clear glass container for each group of students.(Do *not* put lids on the containers.)

2. If you will be using pictures, obtain library books or cut out photos from magazines. You will need pictures of at least two different fish for each group of students.

3. Draw a generalized diagram of a fish on the chalkboard, as shown.

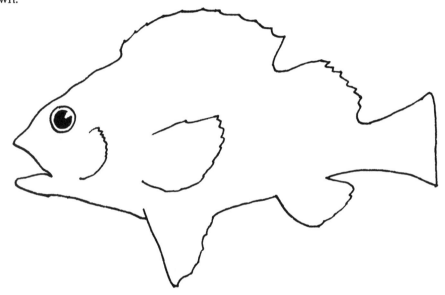

4. Organize the art supplies for easy distribution during the lesson.

5. Add water to the tempera paint until it resists crayon lines when painted over crayon on paper. If the paint is too thick, it will cover the crayon.

6. Tape the large sheet of butcher paper to the front wall or chalkboard.

7. Cover a table with newspaper. Place several containers of tempera paint around the table, along with brushes and containers of clean water. Students will do the first stage of the activity, the drawing, at their desks, and then come to the paint table.

8. Set aside an area of the room where the fish paintings can dry.

9. Arrange to have adult or older student volunteers assist with stuffing, stapling, and hanging the fish after the paintings have dried.

Observing, Comparing, and Describing

1. Ask students to tell you what they know about fish. The following questions are useful in guiding discussion:

How are fish different from other animals? (*Fish live in water and use gills to breathe.*)

How do fish move? (*They use their tails and fins to swim.*)

How do they eat? (*They gulp their food whole or take big bites of food.*)

What body parts does a fish have? (*Body, tail, fins, gills, eyes, scales, etc.*)

2. Review the concept of *structure* with students. Write the word *structure* on the chalkboard, and remind them that the parts of an object or animal form its structure. Explain that today they will be comparing the structure of two different kinds of fish.

3. Draw students' attention to the generalized drawing of a fish on the chalkboard. Ask students whether they know the names of any of the body parts shown, and label the following: mouth, eye, gill, tail, fins, and scales.

4. Explain that every kind of fish is a little different in structure. For instance, some fish have small fins, others have large ones. Tell students that they will be working in groups to compare two kinds of fish. Their job will be to find ways in which the fish are the same, and ways in which they are different.

5. Draw a vertical line down the center of the butcher paper. On one side, write the heading "SAME," and on the other side, write "DIFFERENT." Tell students that after they have investigated the two fish, the class will list the things that are the same about them and the things that are different.

For Grades 2–3: Distribute Activity Sheet 6: Looking at Fish, and tell students to generate lists of similarities and differences in their groups. Later, a reporter from each group can share the group's conclusions.

6. Distribute a goldfish and a guppy to each group of students. (Or, if you are using pictures, distribute them.) The following questions are useful in guiding observation:

How many fins does each fish have? (*5 to 8, depending on species*)

How are the fins the same? Different? (*They all are translucent; they are of different shapes.*)

How are their tails the same? Different? (*They are in same position on the body; they are of different shapes.*)

note

Students should be organized in groups of four for the lesson.

note

Some of the questions ask students to notice movement. Omit such questions if you are using pictures instead of live fish.

How do the two fish move in the water? How are their movements the same? Different? (*They swim; both move their bodies back and forth; guppies are faster.*)

What do their gills look like? (*Slits*)

What colors do you see on each fish? Do they have the same colors, or are they different? (*Each fish has a different pattern of colors.*)

How are their eyes the same or different? (*Both are dark; those of goldfish are larger.*)

How do they move their mouths? How are their movements the same? Different? (*They open and close their mouths; goldfish mouth is opened and closed in a circle; guppy mouth is on top of head area and is not opened and closed as much.*)

7. Give each group a small amount of fish food to feed the fish. Ask students to notice similarities or differences in the way the two fish eat.

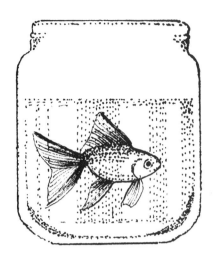

Drawing Conclusions

1. Ask a reporter from each group to share their observations. Record these on the butcher paper.

2. Explain that most fish live in water, have scales, use fins for locomotion, breathe through gills, and hatch from eggs laid in the water. Fish feel cool to the touch because they are cold-blooded—their body temperature is nearly the same as the temperature of their environment. Tell students that animals with these characteristics are called fish.

Creating

1. Tell students that they will use their knowledge of fish body parts to make beautiful fish mobiles.

2. Demonstrate the procedure:

For Kindergarten–Grade 1: Show students two copies of Activity Sheet 7: Fish Outline. Point to each body part, and have students name it: tail, fins, head, and mouth.

On each of the two fish outlines, use a crayon to draw an eye. Next, draw curving or semicircular lines to indicate scales. Use lines to fill in the fins. Add the gills. Ask students what other designs you could draw on the body of the fish.

As you draw, press hard with the crayon. Tell students that their lines should be dark and thick. Use a variety of colors as you draw.

note
Modifications for grades 2–3 are described on the next page.

When the drawings are finished, show students how to take a brush and paint over the entire surface of each sheet with tempera paint. Have students notice that the paint resists the crayon. Tell students that this technique is called *crayon resist.*

Distribute materials so that students can begin working. Circulate, and offer assistance when needed.

When the paintings have dried, have students cut out their fish and write their names on the tail of each one.

For Grades 2–3: Show students how to put two sheets of construction paper together, one on top of the other. Next, draw a large oval shape on the top sheet. This represents the body of the fish.

Ask students to name the fish body parts, and add them as they are named: tail, fins, gill, scales, mouth, eye.

Ask students what other designs they could add to the body of the fish. Explain that as they draw, they must press hard with the crayon to make thick, dark lines. Tell students to use a variety of colors as they draw.

When the drawing is finished, show students how to cut out the fish, holding the two sheets of construction paper together. Duplicate the fish drawing on the second sheet of construction paper. Tell students to write their names on the tail of each fish cutout.

Next, take a brush and paint over both fish surfaces with tempera paint. Have students notice that the paint resists the crayon. Tell students that this technique is called *crayon resist.*

3. Distribute materials so that students can begin working. Circulate, and offer assistance as needed.

Final Touches

Have volunteers help assemble the fish:

Take two matching fish and turn them over so that the white sides face up.

Loosely crumple a piece of facial tissue, and place it in the center of one of the fish. Position the matching fish over the first so that the tissue is between them and the painted sides face outward.

Staple around the edges of the fish to close.

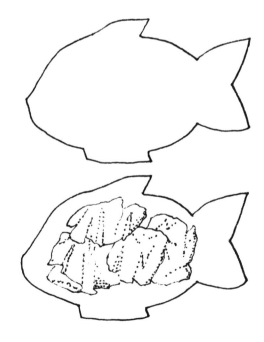

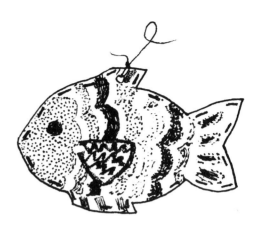

Use the hole punch to put a hole in the top center of the fish. Thread a piece of string or yarn through the hole and tie.

Hang the fish from the ceiling.

Evaluating

Display the finished mobiles. Have students notice the variety of lines and colors used by their peers. Ask volunteers to share one thing they particularly like about their mobiles.

Going Further

- Students can investigate the effect of gravity on fish. Place a fish in a clear, water-filled container with a secure lid, such as an empty peanut butter jar. Ask students to predict what will happen to the fish when you carefully turn the jar upside down. Experiment to discover the result. (Return the fish to the aquarium when you have finished.)

- Students can learn about the various habitats of fish: oceans, lakes, and streams. They can apply what they have learned in creating a mural (see Lesson 21, "Creating Ecosystem Murals" on page 85.)

Additional Resources

Alexander, Kay. "Fantastic Fishes," in *Learning to Look and Create: The Spectra Program, Grade Two.* Palo Alto, Calif.: Dale Seymour, 1987.

Amosky, J. *Freshwater Fish and Fishing.* New York: Four Winds Press, 1982.

Kramer, David C. "Fish," in *Animals in the Classroom*. Menlo Park, Calif.: Addison-Wesley, 1989.

Sisson, Edith A. "Activities With Fish," in *Nature With Children of All Ages.* New York: Prentice-Hall, 1982.

Investigating Leaves Through Printmaking

Overview

In this activity, students learn that leaves come in many different shapes and sizes. They observe the structure of a leaf—its stem, veins, and epidermis. Finally, they make rubbings of leaf shapes with wax crayon and emphasize the design with a contrasting background of tempera paint.

Student Objectives

- identify the parts of a leaf: stem, veins, and epidermis.

- observe that leaves come in many different shapes and sizes.

- understand that rubbings are images made by rubbing wax crayon over paper that has been placed over a textured surface.

- use wax crayon to make rubbings of leaf shapes.

Materials

- collection of various kinds of leaves, preferably sturdy ones with prominent veins, 4 per student

- white construction paper, 12" x 18", 1 per student.

- wax crayons with the paper removed

- newspaper to cover work areas

- (optional) Activity Sheet 8: Looking at Leaves (page 133)

- brushes

- tempera paint in assorted colors

- containers to hold the tempera paint, 1 container per group of students

Getting Ready

1. Organize leaves, paper, and crayons for easy distribution during the lesson.

2. Cover work surfaces with newspaper.

3. Organize students into pairs or groups for the lesson.

4. Set aside an area of the room where the finished rubbings can dry.

Observing, Comparing, and Describing

1. Ask students to close their eyes and to imagine they are looking at a leaf. Have them describe what they see in their mind's eye. Help them provide detailed descriptions by asking questions such as:

What color is the leaf you imagine?

What shape is it? Long or short? Fat or thin?

2. Tell students that you are going to give each of them a real leaf to examine very carefully. They should try to notice as much as they can about its structure. Remind students that the parts of the leaf form its *structure*.

3. Distribute the same kind of leaf so that every student has one. Allow time for investigation. The following questions are useful in guiding observation:

How can you describe the shape of this leaf? The color? (*Answers will vary.*)

What does the leaf feel like? (*Smooth or rough*)
Does the bottom feel the same as the top? (*Veins usually protrude more on the bottom.*)
How does the stem feel? (*Stem may feel smooth or rough.*)

What kinds of lines can you see on the leaf? How do the lines form a pattern? (*The lines, called veins, may be parallel or branching.*)

4. Have students share their observations, and list these on the chalkboard.

5. Explain that the surface of the leaf is called the *epidermis*. The *stem* helps support the leaf and attach it to the plant or tree. The lines running through the leaf are called *veins*. They help carry water and nutrients through the leaf.

6. Give each student three additional leaves, each different. Ask the class to notice ways in which the leaves are the same, and ways in which they are different. Allow time for investigation.

7. Optional: Second- and third-grade students can work in pairs or groups to record their observations on Activity Sheet 8: Looking at Leaves.

Drawing Conclusions

Have students share their observations. Help them understand that although all leaves have an epidermis, stem, and veins, different kinds of leaves can vary in shape, arrangement of veins, and stem structure.

Creating

1. Tell students that the veins on a leaf give the leaf texture. Explain that *texture* is the way something feels, whether it is soft, smooth, prickly, bumpy, and so on. Artists can use things that have texture, like leaves, to make rubbings. Rubbings are images made by stroking wax crayon over paper that has been placed over a textured surface.

2. Demonstrate the procedure:

Place a leaf, underside up, on the table. Explain that the veins are more prominent on the underside.

Cover the leaf with a sheet of white construction paper. Rub the side of a crayon lightly over the paper to find the leaf. Then, holding the leaf in place with one hand, stroke firmly over the surface in one direction, away from your hand. When the leaf's shape and veins are clearly visible, move the leaf to another position, or select another kind of leaf, and repeat the procedure on another part of the paper.

Tell students to make enough rubbings to fill the page, leaving some space between leaves.

Show students how to take a brush, dip it into the tempera, and wipe the excess against the edge of the container. Use a contrasting color of tempera paint to paint in the background around the leaf rubbings.

3. When students understand the procedure, distribute materials so that they can begin to work. Circulate, and offer assistance as necessary.

Evaluating

Display the finished rubbings. Have students notice the contrast of crayon rubbing and painted background. Ask them to identify the leaf parts visible in the rubbings—stems, veins, and leaf edges.

Going Further

■ Have students collect and press a variety of leaves. These may be preserved under clear adhesive paper on a white construction paper background. Challenge students to find a way to classify their leaf collection.

■ Have students observe clover leaves to see how they are affected by sunlight. During the day students will notice that the leaves spread out and change position. At night the leaflets close. The effect of night can be simulated by covering a clover plant with a large can or box. The leaves will begin to close in about a half hour.

Additional Resources

Alexander, Kay. "Crayon-Resist Rubbings," in *Learning to Look and Create: The Spectra Program, Grade One.* Palo Alto, Calif.: Dale Seymour, 1987.

Sisson, Edith A. "Activities With Trees," in *Nature With Children of All Ages.* New York: Prentice-Hall, 1982.

note to kindergarten teachers

You may wish to omit this stage of the art activity, in which students paint a tempera background around their leaf rubbings. Some kindergartners have difficulty controlling the paintbrush and may find the task frustrating.

Investigating Flowers Through Drawing

Overview

In this activity, students examine a variety of flowers and compare their color, shape, and number of petals. Using what they have learned about the structure of flowers, they create crayon or felt-tip pen drawings of as many different flower forms as possible.

Student Objectives

- observe that different kinds of flowers vary in structure.

- use crayons or felt-tip pens to create a drawing using a variety of flower shapes.

Materials

- a variety of flowers for students to examine, at least 4 kinds per group

- colored felt-tip pens or crayons

- large white construction paper, 18" x 11", 1 sheet per student

- *For kindergarten–grade 1:* large sheet of butcher paper, masking tape, and markers

- *For grades 2–3:* Activity Sheet 9: Looking at Flowers (page 134)

- pencils

Getting Ready

1. Collect, or have students collect, a variety of flowers to examine, such as roses, daisies, dandelions, and assorted wildflowers. Flowers may be placed in jars of water until ready to use in the lesson.

2. Organize drawing paper and pens or crayons for easy distribution during the lesson.

3. For Kindergarten–Grade 1: Use a marker to draw six large circles on the butcher paper, as shown. Place the paper on the floor in an area of the room where students can sit in a circle around it.

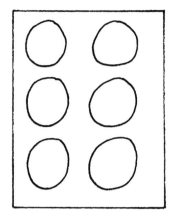

Observing, Comparing, and Describing

For Kindergarten–Grade 1:

1. Ask students to tell what they know about flowers. Questions to guide discussion include:

What color can a flower be? (*Almost any color*)

How many petals can a flower have? (*Almost any number*)

What shapes can a flower's petals have? (*Any number of shapes*)

How large can a flower be? How small? (*From larger than a human hand to small enough to be barely seen*)

2. Have students sit in a large circle on the floor around the butcher paper. Give each student three different kinds of flowers, not all the same color.

3. Ask students to look carefully at their three flowers and to notice how they are different. Allow time for sharing.

4. Tell students that one way the flowers differ is by color. Show students how to classify flowers by color, using the large circles to separate the different groupings. For example, you might say, "I have two yellow flowers and one white one. I can place the yellow flowers in this circle and the white flower in another circle over here."

5. Help one third of the students place their flowers on the butcher paper, grouping them by color. Encourage the rest of the students to observe the classification process carefully and offer suggestions. When all the flowers have been placed in the appropriate circles, remove them and set them aside.

6. Tell students that another way flowers differ is by numbers of petals. Some have three or four, or even more than ten. Help another third of the students place their flowers on the paper, grouping them by the number of petals. When all the flowers have been placed on the paper, remove them and set them aside.

7. Help the remaining students classify their flowers using another criterion, such as size (large, medium, small) or petal shape (long, short, skinny, fat, and so on).

For Grades 2–3:

1. Ask students to tell what they know about flowers. Questions to guide discussion include:

What color can a flower be? (*Almost any color*)

How many petals can a flower have? (*Almost any number*)

What shapes can a flower's petals have? (*Any number of shapes*)

note

Second- and third-grade students should be organized into pairs or groups for this activity.

How large can a flower be? How small? (*From larger than a human hand to small enough to be barely seen*)

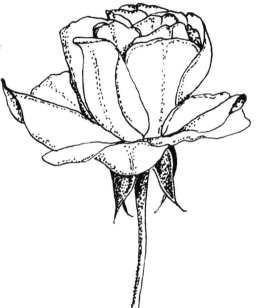

2. Explain that students will be working with a partner or in a group to compare four different kinds of flowers. They should try to notice ways in which the flowers are the same in structure (shape, color, size) and ways in which they are different.

3. Distribute Activity Sheet 9: Looking at Flowers, and show students how to record their observations.

4. Distribute four flowers to each pair or group of students. As students work, circulate, and offer assistance as needed. Additional questions to guide observation include:

How are the colors of the flowers the same? How are they different? Do some flowers have more than one color on their petals? (*Answers will vary depending on the species.*)

How are the petals of the flowers the same? How are they different? Which flower has the longest petals? The shortest? The widest? The narrowest?

How are the centers of the flowers similar or different?

Drawing Conclusions

Draw students together to share their observations. Have students share both similarities and differences among various kinds of flowers.

Creating

1. Tell students that they will now create a drawing that has as many different kinds of flowers as possible. When an artist draws an object in as many different forms as possible, he or she creates a design called a *variation on a theme*.

2. On a large sheet of white construction paper, show students how to outline several large flowers in pencil. As you complete the first flower, ask students how the second could be drawn differently. Tell students that the entire sheet of construction paper should be covered with flowers.

3. Once the pencil outline has been completed, demonstrate how to use crayon or colored felt-tip pen to color in the shapes.

4. When students understand the procedure, distribute materials so that they can begin to work. Circulate, and offer assistance when needed.

Evaluating

Display the finished drawings. Help students notice the variety of form and color used by their classmates. Ask volunteers to share one thing they like about their own or another student's drawing.

Going Further

- Have students collect and press a variety of flowers. After they have been pressed and left to dry, the flowers may be placed between two sheets of wax paper, covered with several sheets of newspaper, and pressed with a warm iron. The finished products may be hung up in a window for display.

- In spring, bring twigs with spring buds to class. Have students open the buds and count the tiny petals inside, using hand lenses for magnification.

- Older students can use reference books to learn about the different state flowers. Have students locate their state flower outdoors and draw pictures of it.

Additional Resources

Alexander, Kay. "A Picture of a Pitcher of Flowers," in *Learning to Look and Create: The Spectra Program, Grade Two.* Palo Alto, Calif.: Dale Seymour, 1987.

Kirkpatrick, Rena K. *Look at Flowers.* Milwaukee: Raintree, 1985.

Interactions

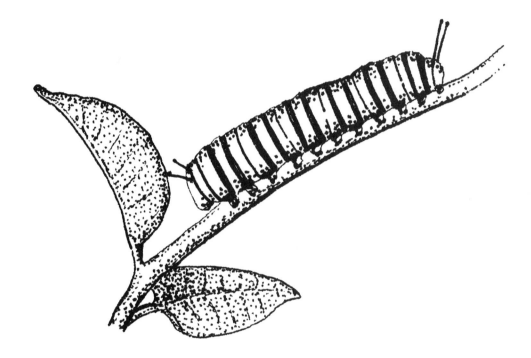

The Theme of Interaction

The investigations in this section are organized around the theme of interactions. *Interactions* are defined as "mutual or reciprocal actions or influences." By exploring interactions within the disciplines of biology, geology, and physics, students learn about the many different kinds of interactions in systems.

Students learn about the interaction of a species with its environment by observing snails in their natural habitat and in the classroom. By baking cookies and watching raw dough rise and solidify, students observe the results of both physical and chemical interactions among atoms and molecules.

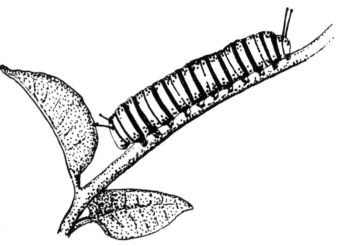

As artists, students learn to experiment with the interactions of different arts media to create new forms and designs. By painting with watercolor over paper that has been partially covered with wax crayon, students explore the interaction of paint with paper and wax. Students learn about the interaction of different pigments as they combine primary colors to create secondary colors.

Introduction to Interactions: Color Combinations

Overview

In this activity, students experiment with the interactions of primary colors in pigments. Using small sponges, students mix tempera paint to produce the colors of leaves and stamp-print the leafy parts of trees.

Student Objectives

- understand that an interaction occurs when living or nonliving things affect or change each other in some way.

- predict and observe the interaction of pigments to produce new colors.

- use the media skills of color mixing and stamp-printing to create pictures of trees.

Materials

- manila or colored construction paper for background, 12" x 18", 1 sheet per student

- cellulose sponges cut into 5–6 small squares, 1" or so

- spring-type clothespins as handles for sponge pieces

- low containers for paint, such as cut-off milk cartons

- tempera paint: red, blue, yellow, brown

- paper plates or aluminum trays for mixing colors, 3 per group

- plastic teaspoons, 1 per container of red, blue, and yellow paint

- short (2" x 3" x 1") lengths of cardboard

- newspapers to cover tables

- several leaves of different colors

- (optional) Activity Sheet 10: Color Mixing (page 135)

Getting Ready

1. For Kindergarten–Grade 1: Sketch three large circles or ovals on each sheet of background paper to serve as guides for the leafy parts of three trees.

2. Attach clothespins to sponge pieces as handles. Allow two to three sponges per container.

3. Each group of three students should have a container each of red, yellow, and blue paint and one paper plate per student. Place one plastic teaspoon into each container.

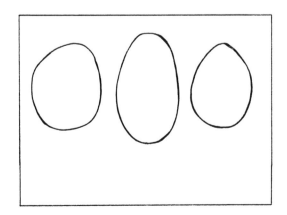

4. Put a few tablespoons of brown tempera in containers so that each group of students will have one. Cut three to four cardboard pieces to use with each container of brown paint.

5. Cover work areas with newspaper, and arrange printing materials for easy distribution.

Observing, Comparing, and Describing

1. Show students several leaves, and ask how their colors differ. Ask, "What other colors can leaves be?" Allow time for sharing.

2. Show students the containers of red, yellow, and blue paint, and explain that these are called *primary colors*. Tell students that when these colors are mixed together, they interact to create other colors, such as green, orange, purple, brown, and black.

3. Help students understand that an *interaction* occurs when two or more things affect or change each other in some way. Ask, "What do you predict, or guess, the interaction of red and yellow will be? The interaction of red and blue? Of blue and yellow? Encourage students to use the word *interaction* in their answers, as in, "I think the interaction of red and yellow will be orange."

Creating

1. Explain that you are going to demonstrate the interaction of blue and yellow paint. Show how to use the teaspoon to spoon a small amount of yellow paint onto a paper mixing plate. Use another teaspoon to add a small amount of blue to the yellow. Tell students that they should always add the darker color to the lighter.

2. Next, use the clothespin holder to stamp the sponge into the paint, mixing the color. Add a little more blue and mix again. Have students notice that the green becomes more intense as more blue is added.

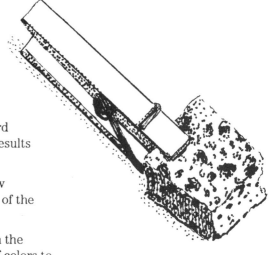

3. On a large sheet of construction paper for the background, show students how to stamp-print the leafy part of one tree. Dip a sponge into the green paint, wipe it on the edge of the container, and print a large circular or oval shape on one third of the paper. Do not cover the paper too thickly—keep the results airy and open.

4. Take a piece of small cardboard, turn it on its edge, and show students how to dip it into the brown tempera. Use the edge of the cardboard to stamp a trunk and branches.

5. Point out that you still have room to make two more trees on the paper. Tell students that they can mix other combinations of colors to make leaves for the remaining trees.

6. Demonstrate how to use the sponges to mix and stamp orange and purple leaves.

7. Explain that once a sponge has been used to mix a color, that sponge should always be used to mix more of the same color. A sponge that has been used to mix green must be left on the green mixing plate when students are finished with it.

8. Have the class begin printing the leaves, trunks, and branches of their trees. Circulate, and offer assistance where needed.

Drawing Conclusions

When students have finished, gather them together to review what they have learned. Ask, "How do different colors interact with each other? How does an artist mix green? (*Blue and yellow*) Orange? (*Red and yellow*) Purple? (*Red and blue*)"

Explaining the Phenomenon

Explain the phenomenon to older students:

We are able to see colors because of the light that is reflected from an object's surface. Certain materials absorb more light than others. Different-colored paints are made of different kinds of materials that absorb light differently.

Light is made up of different colors, as in a rainbow. Red paint looks red because the blue, green, and yellow light is absorbed and the red light is reflected by the pigment in the paint. When two colors are mixed, their pigments interact to form a material that absorbs light differently than the original colors.

Evaluating

Display the finished stamp prints for everyone to see. Discuss the similarities between the prints and the appearance of living trees. How do the ways students made the branches differ? Does every print look the same? What did the artists do to make their prints unique?

Going Further

- Students can investigate the absorption of light by different colors of construction paper. On a sunny day, tape sheets of different-colored construction paper on the asphalt or concrete outside the classroom. Remind students that different colors reflect light differently.

  Have students predict which color will reflect the most light. Tell students that they will be able to actually feel the differences, since colors that reflect most of the light feel cooler than colors that absorb most of the light.

  Let students investigate the sheets of colored paper. Ask them to discover which color reflects the most light. Have them work with partners to try to order the colors from most to least reflective.

- Second- and third-grade students can extend their investigation of color combinations using sets of watercolors and Activity Sheet 10: Color Mixing.

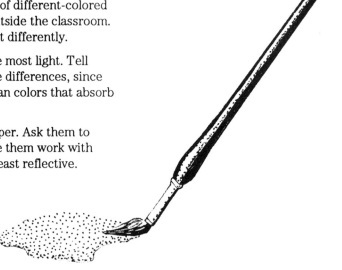

Additional Resources

Alexander, Kay. "Orange Caterpillars" and "Tree Shapes," in *Learning to Look and Create: The Spectra Program, Kindergarten.* Palo Alto, Calif.: Dale Seymour, 1989.

Investigating Evaporation with Watercolors

Overview

In this activity, students make predictions, conduct experiments, and draw conclusions about the process of evaporation. They observe that the interaction of heat and water increases the speed of evaporation. After using wet-in-wet techniques with watercolors, students observe the effects of evaporation on the colors and patterns in their paintings.

Student Objectives

- observe that water can change its state from a liquid to a gas.

- observe that evaporation increases when an inter- action takes place between water and moving air.

- create paintings using wet-in-wet watercolor techniques and observe the color patterns left behind when the water evaporates.

Materials

- newspapers to cover work areas

- sponge

- piece of cardboard, approximately 10" square

- large flat paintbrushes, 1 per student

- containers to hold water

- 8 1/2" x 11" sheets of watercolor paper, or white construction paper

- small watercolor brushes, 1 per student

- watercolors, 1 set or several individual pans per student

- timer

Getting Ready

1. Set aside an area of the room where completed paintings can dry undisturbed.

2. Organize painting materials for easy distribution during the lesson.

3. Cover work surfaces with newspaper.

4. Wet the sponge and place it near the front chalkboard.

Observing, Comparing, and Describing

1. Begin by having students share their knowledge of evaporation. The following questions are useful in guiding discussion:

Have you ever noticed the puddles on streets and sidewalks after it rains? What happens to the water as puddles disappear? (*Goes into the air*)

How long does it take your hair to dry after you have washed it? (*Answers will vary.*) What can you do to make your hair dry faster? (*Use a hairdryer, stand in the sun, etc.*)

2. Use the wet sponge to make two wet marks, several feet apart, on the chalkboard. Make each mark approximately 1 foot long. Point to one of the marks and ask, "What could I do to make this wet mark dry faster than the other?" (*Blow on it, fan it, etc.*) Allow time for sharing.

3. Use the piece of cardboard to fan one of the marks several times. Call on student volunteers to take turns fanning until the mark has *evaporated*. Have students notice that applying a breeze to the wet surface caused the water to disappear more quickly.

Drawing Conclusions

1. Ask students why the water mark under the cardboard fan disappeared more quickly than the other water mark. Allow time for students to share their ideas.

2. Explain that when water changes to a gas, the process is called *evaporation*. When water evaporates, it changes into a gas and seems to disappear. When a breeze, or moving air, passes over the surface of the water, the rate of evaporation will increase. Heat will also increase the rate of evaporation.

Explaining the Phenomenon

Explain the phenomenon to older students:

Water is made up of tiny molecules. Each molecule contains two hydrogen atoms and one oxygen atom. The molecules of water are always in motion. At the surface of the water, the molecules travel in every possible direction. Attractions from nearby molecules within the water keep most of the molecules at the surface from leaving. When some molecules head almost straight out from the surface, they escape into the air in the process called *evaporation*.

Creating

1. Tell students that artists mix watercolor paints with water to create paintings on paper. As the water on the paper evaporates, the colors are left behind.

2. Demonstrate the procedure:

Dip a large, clean paintbrush into clear water. Using broad, horizontal strokes, completely wet the surface of an 8 1/2" x 11" paper.

Dip a smaller brush into the water. Work the wet brush against the surface of a watercolor pan to load color onto the brush. Dab the loaded brush against the wet paper so that a patch of color spreads out and bleeds onto the surface.

Rinse the brush thoroughly.

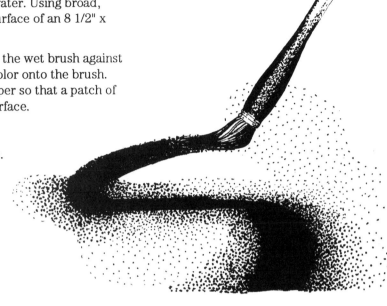

Repeat the process with two more colors. Continue loading the brush and dabbing the paper until the entire surface is covered with color. Occasionally dab one color into another so that the colors combine on the paper.

Explain as you work that this kind of painting is called *wet-in-wet water-color painting*, because wet color is added to the wet surface of the paper.

3. When students understand the procedure, distribute materials and let them begin. Circulate, and offer assistance when needed.

Observing, Comparing, and Describing

When students are finished, set the paintings aside to dry. At regular 15-minute intervals, let students take a look at their paintings to see how much of the water has evaporated and to notice how evaporation has affected the colors and patterns on the paper. Questions to guide discussion include:

How do the colors change when they dry? (*They become less bright.*)

What marks or patterns can you find in your painting that were caused by evaporation? (*Students will notice the outlines of former puddles.*)

Evaluating

Display the finished, dried paintings. Ask volunteers to share one thing they like about their painting. Help students notice interesting marks or patterns created by evaporation.

Going Further

- Students can gain an idea of the extent of evaporation going on all the time by experimenting with wet paper towels. Wet several towels thoroughly, and squeeze them out so that they will not drip. Have students hang them in selected areas indoors and outdoors and note the order in which the towels dry out.

■ Students can experiment with the cooling effect of evaporation. Have students blow on their index fingers. Then have them dip their index fingers into water and blow again. Their fingers will feel cool. Help students understand that as the water evaporates, it needs heat and takes up heat from its surroundings, namely, their index fingers. Point out that evaporation of perspiration keeps their bodies cool. The more quickly the perspiration evaporates, the more quickly it takes heat from their bodies and the cooler they feel.

■ Students can use wet-in-wet techniques to paint beautiful sunsets. First, demonstrate how to wet the paper thoroughly. Then load yellow color onto a brush, and drag it horizontally across the bottom third of the paper. Next, load the brush with orange, and drag it horizontally just above the yellow so that the colors overlap slightly. Repeat the process with red, then purple, and then blue. After the colors have dried, students can use dark blue or black paint to create a mountain silhouette across the bottom of the paper.

Additional Resources

Alexander, Kay. "A Forest and Its Trees," in *Learning to Look and Create: The Spectra Program, Grade Three.* Palo Alto, Calif.: Dale Seymour, 1987.

Lowery, Lawrence F. "Meteorology," in *The Everyday Science Sourcebook.* Palo Alto, Calif.: Dale Seymour, 1985.

Exploring Sticky and Smooth with Monoprints

Overview

Why do some materials stick to others? In this activity, students compare the interaction of different materials and categorize them according to degree of adhesiveness. They then use the adhesive properties of finger paint to create monoprints from original finger-painted images.

Student Objectives

- observe and compare the adhesive properties, or stickiness, of various liquid and solid materials.

- create a monoprint from an original finger-painted image.

Materials

- a variety of sticky and nonsticky liquids and solids for each group of students, such as: bits of modeling clay, cotton balls, scraps of fabric or paper, several kinds of tape, scraps of Velcro™, paste, honey, liquid starch, water, and pebbles.

- containers to hold the liquids and solids at each table

- damp paper towels or rags for wiping fingers

- *For grades 2–3:* Activity Sheet 11: How Sticky Is It? (page 136), 1 per group

- masking tape

- sheets of butcher paper, 18" x 24", or sheets of glossy finger-paint paper

- powdered tempera paint

- liquid starch

- smocks for students

- old towels and sponges for cleanup

Getting Ready

1. For each group of four students, organize a collection of sticky and nonsticky liquids and solids in small containers. Dampen several paper towels or old rags for every group so that students

note

Students should be organized in groups of four for this lesson. During the art activity, only four students will create monoprints at a time. Independent activities for the rest of the class are suggested in step 5 on page 58.

can wipe their fingers after testing each of the materials.

2. Organize the collection of solids and liquids, damp rags, and activity sheets for easy distribution during the lesson.

3. Select a table for the printing activity. The table should be close to a water source, such as a sink or bucket. Affix masking tape to the surface around several rectangular areas approximately 18" x 24" Place finger-paint paper nearby, along with containers of powdered tempera and liquid starch.

4. Set aside an area of the room where finished monoprints can lie flat or hang to dry.

5. Arrange to have a parent volunteer or upper-grade student help with the printing activity, especially if you are teaching kindergarten or first grade.

Observing, Comparing, and Describing

1. Ask students whether they have ever touched something that was really sticky. Allow time for sharing.Questions to guide discussion include:

What is the stickiest thing you have ever felt? (*Answers will vary.*)

What sticky things do we have in the classroom? (*Masking tape, glue, modeling clay, etc.*)

What is the least sticky, or smoothest, thing you have ever felt? (*Answers will vary.*)

2. Show students a collection of liquids and solids. Hold up one item at a time, and have students predict whether it will be sticky or smooth. Ask students to predict which items will be the stickiest.

3. Demonstrate how to test each item. Place the tip of your index inger into one of the liquids. Press the liquid between the tips of your thumb and index finger to test its stickiness, then use a damp paper towel to wipe your fingers clean.

4. For Grades 2–3: Show students Activity Sheet 11: How Sticky Is It? Tell them to test all of the items first and then to decide as a group which was stickiest, which was second stickiest, and so on. Demonstrate how to rank the items on the activity sheet from very sticky to very smooth. Explain that each group will be given only one activity sheet, so they should choose a group member to do the writing.

5. When students understand the procedure, distribute the materials, and have them begin. Circulate, and offer assistance when needed.

Drawing Conclusions

1. Have a student from each group share observations and rankings.

2. Help students speculate about what causes something to be either sticky or smooth. Have them discuss the differences between sticky and smooth items.

Explaining the Phenomenon

1. Explain that liquids and solids are made up of tiny particles called *atoms* and *molecules*. In some materials, the atoms and molecules may interact with the atoms and molecules of another material. Write the word *interaction* on the chalkboard. Remind students that an interaction occurs when two or more things affect or change each other in some way.

2. Have students simulate molecular attraction through role-play. Ask for two volunteers to come to the front of the class. Select one student to role-play a glue molecule, and the other student to role-play a paper molecule. Have the volunteers stand about 10 feet apart with their arms stretched out in front of them. Ask them to walk slowly toward each other and to be ready to clasp hands as soon as they are able. Tell students that the interaction that occurs between glue and paper is an attraction between the molecules of the glue and the molecules of the paper.

3. Ask for two additional volunteers to come up to the front of the class. Have them role-play the molecules of two pebbles. Ask them to stand about 10 feet apart with their arms clasped tightly about their chests. Have them slowly walk toward each other until they bump gently into each other and then walk away. Tell students that the attraction between these two molecules is not enough for them to stick to each other.

4. Explain that scientists call the stickiness, or attraction, of certain molecules *adhesion*. Adhesive materials, such as glues and tapes, are useful in holding things together.

Creating

1. Tell students that finger paints are made with liquid starch, which causes them to be fairly sticky, or adhesive. The adhesiveness of finger paints makes them very useful in creating a special kind of print, called a *monoprint*.

2. Explain that *mono* means "one," and that each monoprint is the only one of its kind.

3. In front of the entire class, demonstrate the procedure with a student partner:

Pour some liquid starch into the center of one of the taped areas on the surface of the printing table. Spread the starch with one hand until the entire area is covered.

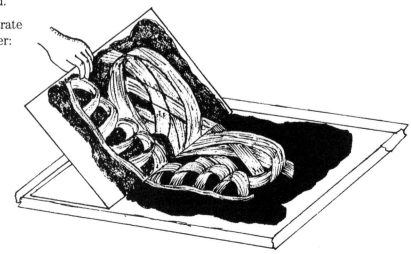

Sprinkle a color of powdered tempera over it, and use your fingers to mix it with the starch. Use fingers, fingernails, and palms to create lines, shapes, and textures in the finger paint.

Have a student partner lay a sheet of paper over the paint. As your partner firmly presses the back of the paper all over, wipe the paint from your hands with a damp sponge or rag.

Gently peel the print from the table surface, and lay it aside to dry.

4. Explain that partners will take turns; on one turn, a student will finger-paint, and on the next turn, he or she will help the partner make the monoprint.

5. Tell the class that everyone will have a chance to work with a partner to create a monoprint, but that only a small group of students can be at the printing table at a time. Select a group of four students to begin working on their monoprints while you engage the rest of the class in a related activity, such as helping students:

   ▪ list as many sticky foods as they can. These may be categorized in groups, such as "yummy" or "yucky."

   ▪ create a small book of "Sticky Things," with an illustration or description of a sticky item on each page.

   ▪ write a story or draw a picture about what it would be like to land on a planet whose surface was covered with glue. Have students design a spaceship capable of leaving such a surface.

6. As students finish their monoprints, have them join the class in the related activity, and select others to go to the printing table in their place.

Evaluating

1. Display the finished prints. Have students notice similarities and differences in the prints, pointing out that no two prints are exactly alike.

2. Help students find a variety of lines and textures in the monoprints.

Going Further

▪ Students can observe the adhesion between water and glass molecules. Have students observe the water in partly filled glass containers, such as jars. Students will notice that the water climbs slightly higher on each side than in the middle. Water molecules adhere better to glass than they cohere to other water molecules; this causes the water to climb the sides of the jar.

■ Have students observe the capillarity of water in celery stalks. Obtain two celery stalks with yellow leaves. Place one stalk, leafy end upward, in red ink or a red food color solution; place the other stalk in a blue solution. Leave them in bright sunlight for a few hours. Students will notice that the colored water has climbed the celery stalk. The water molecules are more attracted to the walls of the celery strings, or pipes, than to other molecules; this causes the water to rise in the stalk.

Additional Resources

Alexander, Kay. "Monoprints," in *Learning to Look and Create: The Spectra Program, Grade One.* Palo Alto, Calif.: Dale Seymour, 1987.

Allison, Linda, and David Katz. "Sticky Fingerprints," in *Gee, Wiz!* Boston: Little, Brown, 1983.

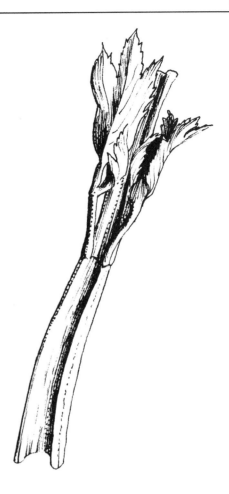

Using Chemistry to Bake a Sculpture

Overview

In this activity, students investigate the properties of raw baker's clay—a mixture of flour, salt, and water. They use such modeling techniques as pinching, rolling, and squeezing to create small sculptures. By observing the properties of the clay after it has been baked in an oven, students learn about the interaction of heat and matter to produce chemical change.

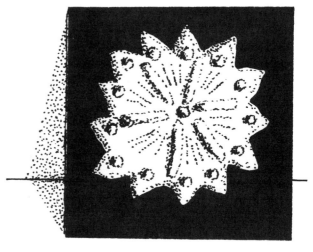

Student Objectives

- understand that the addition of heat to a substance can cause a chemical change.

- observe the change in physical properties that occurs when dough is baked.

- use a variety of techniques to model figures from baker's clay.

Materials

- baker's clay (see recipe below)

- mixing bowl and spoon

- toothpicks

- small, shallow containers of water

- sheets of wax paper to serve as place mats for work areas

- cookie sheets

- *For grades 2–3:* Activity Sheet 12: Looking at Baker's Clay (page 137)

- oven

- paper plates

- (optional) clear varnish to paint or spray finished sculptures; cardboard or corkboard scraps for mounting plaques; white glue

- (optional) Activity Sheet 13: How Does It Change? (page 138)

Getting Ready

1. *Baker's clay recipe*

For each batch, mix 4 cups of flour with 1 cup of salt. Add 1 1/2 cups of water, and stir. Knead thoroughly on a lightly floured surface until the dough is no longer sticky. For colored dough, substitute 1/3 to 1/2 cup of liquid tempera for part of the water. Each batch makes enough dough for 10–12 students to make one or two small figures.

2. Mix the dough on the day it is to be used, since baker's clay can become sticky when stored. The kneading can be done by students.

Observing and Creating

1. Ask students whether they have ever handled raw bread dough or cookie dough. Ask, "What happens to the dough when it is baked in the oven? Does it change in any way?" Allow time for sharing.

2. Tell students that adding heat to the dough causes a special kind of interaction to occur—a *chemical change*. Explain that this chemical change is very useful in cooking and can also be used in making sculptures.

3. Show students a ball of baker's clay. Flatten the ball into a cookie shape. Demonstrate the techniques of rolling, pinching, and squeezing the dough to achieve various shapes. Show how to roll a ball into an elongated shape for an arm, leg, or tree branch.

4. Demonstrate how to join two pieces of clay by putting a drop of water on one piece and then pressing the two pieces together.

5. Show students how to use the end of a toothpick to make small dot patterns on the surface of the clay. Press the side of the toothpick into the clay to create line patterns.

6. Ask students to think of different kinds of figures that can be modeled, such as faces, boats, animals, and abstract shapes. Point out that the finished sculpture should be somewhat flattened, like a cookie, so that it will bake easily.

7. Tell students that as they work with the clay they should observe its structure carefully—its color, shape, size, texture, and weight. Let them know that after their sculptures are finished, you will ask them to share their observations.

8. Distribute materials. Circulate, and offer assistance when needed. Check that sculptures are properly flattened (that is, no thicker than 1/2 inch). Place the finished sculptures on a cookie sheet.

9. Preheat the oven to 325°F (275°F for colored pieces). Bake the sculptures, allowing one-half hour for each one-fourth inch of thickness. Pieces thicker than one-fourth inch should be turned over after the first half-hour. Place the baked sculptures on individual paper plates to cool.

note
You might wish to divide this lesson into two sessions. In the first session, students can investigate raw dough and create sculptures. In the second sesion, after the sculptures are baked, students can make observations and comparisons.

Observing, Comparing, and Describing

1. Bring the class together to discuss the properties of the raw baker's clay. Ask students to share their observations of the clay's texture, shape, colors, and so on. For kindergarten and first-grade students, list the observations on the chalkboard. Have second- and third-grade students work with partners or in small groups to write their observations in the top section of Activity Sheet 12: Looking at Baker's Clay.

2. After the sculptures have baked, have students examine their sculptures to see how they have changed. Ask students to notice differences in size, texture, shape, color, and weight. Demonstrate how to handle a sculpture gently so that it will not break.

3. List the observations of kindergarten and first-grade students on the board. Have second- and third-grade students write their observations on the bottom section of Activity Sheet 12: Looking at Baker's Clay.

note:

Let students know that any breakages can be mended easily with white glue.

Drawing Conclusions

1. Bring the class together for a discussion of what they learned about what happens to dough when it is baked.

2. Help students understand that the baker's clay, like everything else in the world, is made up of tiny particles called *atoms* and *molecules*. When the dough is heated, its molecules begin to move about and to combine in new ways. Although atoms and molecules are too small for us to see, we can observe the result of their new combinations—the soft dough has changed into a hard sculpture.

Evaluating

1. Display the finished sculptures for everyone to see. Have students notice the different techniques that were used. Can they find examples of pinching? Rolling? Making patterns with toothpicks?

2. Ask students to look at their own sculpture and to think of one thing they really like about it. Would they do anything differently if they were to make another one?

Final Touches

1. After the sculptures have been air-dried for a week, either you or an adult volunteer can spray them outside with a clear acrylic varnish to add a glossy shine.

2. Dried sculptures can be mounted on cardboard
or corkboard plaques with white glue. A paper
clip glued to the back of the board will serve as
a hanger.

Going Further

- Ask your students to notice the physical changes
  in different foods during cooking at home. Second-
  and third-grade students can use Activity Sheet 13:
  How Does It Change? to record their observations.

- Have students use colored baker's clay to make
  ornaments. Paper clips can be pushed in to serve
  as hangers. The pieces should be air-dried for a week and
  then painted with clear acrylic varnish to add a glossy shine.

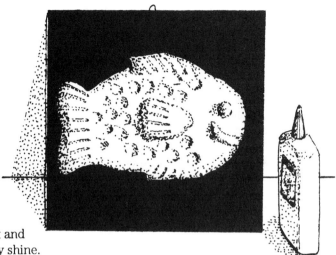

Additional Resources

Alexander, Kay. "Baker's Clay Sculpture," in *Learning to Look and
Create: The Spectra Program, Kindergarten.* Palo Alto, Calif.: Dale
Seymour, 1989.

Exploring Gravity with Splatter Paintings

Overview

In this activity, students investigate the force of gravity by dropping various objects. As the teacher drops small quantities of paint onto a sheet of butcher paper from different heights, students compare the size of the splatters and observe that objects increase in acceleration as they fall to earth. Next, students move outdoors and investigate further on their own as they create multicolored splatter paintings with tempera paint.

Student Objectives

- observe that gravity is a force that can produce motion.

- observe an increase in acceleration as objects fall to earth.

- use tempera paint and the force of gravity to create splatter paintings on colored construction paper.

Materials

- fairly thin, liquid tempera paint in assorted colors

- containers to hold the paint, such as cut-off milk cartons

- plastic straws, several per container of paint

- large sheet of butcher paper and masking tape

- ball, such as a basketball, kickball, or rubber ball

- newspapers

- colored construction paper, 12" x 18"

Getting Ready

1. Add sufficient water to the tempera paint to create a solution that will drop easily from a straw and splatter on paper.

2. Organize art materials for easy distribution during the lesson.

3. Select a space outdoors where students can create their splatter paintings. Although the paint will not splatter up onto students' clothing, small amounts of paint may splatter at ground level a distance of two feet or more from each student's paper. On a day with no wind, you might have students work on a grassy surface. Another solution is to tape large sheets of newspaper to the concrete or blacktop and to have students place their art paper directly in the center of the newspaper.

4. Tape the large sheet of butcher paper to the floor of the classroom where students can see it easily. Place several containers of tempera paint and straws nearby.

Observing, Comparing, and Describing

1. Have a student come to the front of the class and hold up a ball. Ask students to observe carefully as the volunteer bounces the ball several times. The following questions are useful in guiding discussion:

What happens to the ball as it is let go? (*It drops.*)

Why does it fall down? (*Gravity*)

Why doesn't it fall up? (*Gravity*)

2. Have several students come to the front of the class with an object from their desks, such as erasers, crayons, and pencils. Ask the volunteers to hold up their objects and then to let go. Ask the class why the objects fell down rather than up.

3. Explain that a *force* is a push or a pull. *Gravity* is a force that pulls all objects toward the earth. The force of gravity causes everything to fall down and not up.

4. Show students a container of tempera paint. Place one end of a straw in the paint, and cover the other end with your thumb. Remove the straw from the paint, and hold it over the butcher paper. Tell students that when you lift your thumb from the end of the straw, a drop of paint will fall onto the paper. Hold the straw 2 inches above the paper, and ask students to predict what the drop of paint will look like when it hits the paper.

5. Let the drop of paint fall. (It will make a fairly round spot on the paper.) Have students notice its size and appearance.

6. Ask students to predict what the paint will look like if it is dropped from twice as high, say 4 inches. Let the second drop fall next to the first. Again, have students notice its size and appearance.

7. Repeat the procedure, each time increasing the distance that the drop of paint will fall. Students will notice that as the drops fall farther, they create larger spots and begin to splatter across the paper. The size and splattering of the drops will increase the farther the paint falls.

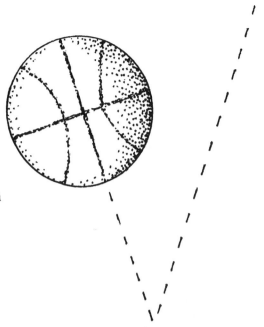

Drawing Conclusions

1. Have students compare the splatters on the butcher paper and discuss the differences. Questions to guide discussion include:

How do the drops change in size? In appearance? (*They become larger and more spread out.*)

What causes the drops to grow larger and splatter when they fall from a greater height? (*They are falling faster and hitting the paper harder.*)

If you jumped down from a height of 2 inches, what would it feel like? (*A gentle bump on landing*) From a height of 2 feet? (*A harder impact*)

2. Help students understand that as objects are pulled to the earth by the force of gravity, they *accelerate*—in other words, they fall faster and faster toward the earth. The faster an object falls, the harder it will hit the ground. The faster a drop of paint is falling, the farther it will splatter when it hits the paper.

Creating

1. Demonstrate the painting technique indoors. Place some newspaper over the sheet of butcher paper on the floor. Lay a sheet of construction paper on the newspaper. Show students how to use the straw to drop various colors of tempera paint on the paper. Vary the height of the straw to release a combination of small, round drops and large, splattered ones.

2. Tell students that they should try to cover the area of the paper with splatters, leaving some of the colored background showing. Explain that the class will be working outdoors.

3. When students understand the procedure, take them outdoors, distribute materials, and have them begin to paint. Circulate, and offer assistance when needed.

Evaluating

Display the dried paintings. Have students compare the size of the splatters used by their classmates. Point out examples of *repetition*, in which students repeated the same size or color of drop throughout their paintings.

Going Further

- Use the splatter paintings in a creative-thinking activity. Show students how to cut out a large shape from their painting. Paste the shape in the center of a sheet of construction paper. Using crayons or felt markers, add legs, arms, and a head to the shape to turn it into an imaginary animal. Help students think of other things they could create from a shape, such as a house, boat, or dinosaur.

- Challenge students to think of ways to overcome gravity or to escape its pull for a while. Point out that jumping is one way to overcome gravity temporarily. Ask them to think of examples in nature in which animals, plants, or other things overcome gravity (for example, birds in flight, floating dandelion seeds, bubbles). Students can record their ideas in a gravity logbook by drawing pictures or writing.

Additional Resources

Allison, Linda, and David Katz. "Splat Testing," in *Gee, Wiz!* Boston: Little, Brown, 1983.

Strongin, Herb. "Overcoming Gravity," in *Science on a Shoestring.* Menlo Park, Calif.: Addison-Wesley, 1991.

Constructing Garbage Structures

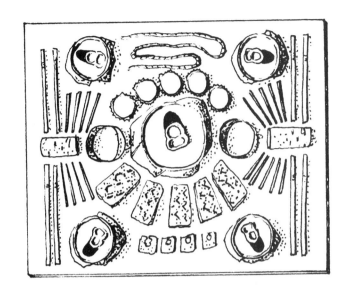

Overview

In this activity, the teacher challenges students to pick up as much litter as they can in 10 minutes. Students work outdoors in teams of four, counting the number of trash items they pick up and observing the kinds of items they find. Then, after a class discussion about the interaction of litter and the environment, students recycle clean trash items from home by using them to create bas-relief sculptures.

Student Objectives

- identify a wide variety of trash items found on the schoolyard, and observe which can be recycled.

- create a bas-relief sculpture with found objects.

- create a design using the elements of repetition and texture.

Materials

- assorted clean throwaway objects, such as scraps of cardboard, toilet paper tubes, paper towel tubes, paper cups, egg cartons, crushed aluminum cans, buttons, scraps of aluminum foil, metal and plastic lids, twists and bread ties, and wire

- white glue

- shallow containers, such as cut-off milk cartons

- newspapers to cover work areas

- sheets of stiff tagboard, 9" x 12", 1 per student

- stiff-bristle brushes, 1" wide

- heavy gloves (e.g., gardening gloves), 1 pair per student

- large trash bags for collecting litter on the schoolyard, 1 per group of 4 students

- (optional) gold or silver enamel spray paint

- (optional) Activity Sheet 14: What's in the Trash? (page 139)

Getting Ready

1. Select an area of the school for the cleanup activity.

2. Have your students begin collecting and cleaning various throwaway objects from home before you start the lesson. A sample letter to parents or guardians, requesting donations, appears on page 151 (bottom).

3. Pour white glue into several shallow containers, one per group of four students. Fill several containers with water. Cover work areas with newspaper.

4. Organize collections of objects into shallow tubs or bags for easy distribution during the lesson, along with the tagboard, stiff-bristle brushes, and glue.

5. Set aside an area of the classroom where the finished sculptures can dry undisturbed.

Predicting

1. Begin by having students share what they know about litter and recycling. The following questions are useful in guiding discussion:

What is litter? (*Trash lying scattered about*)

What kinds of things do we throw away? (*Paper, cans, food scraps, etc.*)

Why is litter harmful? (*It causes pollution; animals sometimes choke on plastic objects.*)

What is recycling? (*Reusing items that otherwise would be thrown away*)

What kinds of things can be recycled? (*Newspaper, cans, glass and plastic bottles, etc.*)

2. Ask students to predict how many pieces of litter they can pick up outside on the schoolyard (or in some other designated area) in 10 minutes. Record predictions on the chalkboard. Ask students to predict the kinds of litter they think they will find, and record these predictions as well.

3. Tell students that they will be working in groups of four to try to pick up as much litter as they can in 10 minutes. Each group will be given a large trash bag to hold the litter. Explain that they should count the number of trash items they pick up and notice the kinds of items they find.

4. When students understand the procedure, distribute heavy gloves and a trash bag to each group, and take the class outdoors to begin the cleanup activity. After 10 minutes, signal the teams to stop collecting. Have students dispose of their trash bags and then wash their hands before returning to the classroom.

Drawing Conclusions

1. Have students share both the number and kind of items they picked up. Help them speculate about the causes and problems of litter. The following questions are useful in guiding discussion:

What was the difference between your prediction and the number of trash items you picked up?

What kinds of litter did you find most often? Least often?

Did different areas have different kinds of litter?

Who do you think is responsible for the litter you found?

note
Students should be organized into groups of four for this activity.

SAFETY TIP
Caution students against picking up any object with a sharp edge.

What would happen if everybody picked up litter in this way each day?

What suggestions do you have for reducing the amount of litter in this area?

2. Tell students that litter occurs in nature, too. In the fall, for example, trees litter the ground with their leaves. Ask students why one kind of litter (playground trash) is considered harmful, while the other (leaves) is not.

3. Help students understand the interaction between litter and the environment. Remind them that an *interaction* occurs when two or more things affect each other in some way. Litter in nature is part of a useful interaction between living things. For instance, leaves decay and leave nutrients in the soil, which nourish the trees. Much of the trash found on the playground, on the other hand, decays very slowly, if at all, and provides no useful nutrients for plants. Plastic is especially long-lasting. A plastic six-pack beverage holder is dangerous to wildlife—many animals have choked to death when their heads catch in the plastic loops.

4. Have students list kinds of litter that can be *recycled*, or used again (paper, aluminum, glass, certain plastics, etc.). Point out that finding alternative uses for things is also a way of recycling. For example, when an artist uses trash items to create a sculpture, he or she is recycling the trash into a work of art.

Creating

1. Tell students that they will create a bas-relief sculpture using throwaway objects. Explain that *bas-relief* (bä´ri lef´) is a sculpture in which the forms project slightly from the surface.

2. Demonstrate the procedure: First, show students a piece of tagboard, and explain that it will serve as the surface for the bas-relief. Arrange a variety of throwaway objects on the tagboard to create an interesting pattern or design. As you work, help students notice how the objects project from the surface. Have them notice examples of repetition in your design. Point out the various textures created by the objects.

3. Tell students that they should experiment with several designs until they are ready to make a final design with glue.

4. Dip a stiff-bristle brush into a container of glue. Using broad, horizontal strokes, cover the surface of the tagboard with a thick layer of glue. Wipe excess glue against the edge of the container, and place the brush, bristles down, into a container of water.

5. Next, arrange the objects in a design on the glue surface. Press each object firmly into the glue.

6. When students understand the procedure, distribute tagboard and collections of throwaway objects. Do not distribute the glue at this time. Allow sufficient time for students to experiment with a variety of designs on the tagboard. Circulate, and offer assistance when needed.

7. When students are ready to create their final designs, distribute the containers of glue, brushes, and water. Encourage students to paint the glue on thickly. Remind them to place their brushes in the water when they have finished with the glue.

Final Touches

1. When the bas-relief sculptures have dried, either you or an adult volunteer can take them outside, place them on newspaper, and spray them with gold or silver enamel paint.

2. Mount the sculptures against a black construction paper background for an attractive bulletin board display.

Evaluating

Display the finished sculptures. Ask students to look for examples of repetition in the bas-reliefs. Help them notice and compare the textures created by various kinds of objects.

Going Further

- Students can experiment to discover what kinds of litter are biodegradable. Have students cut large milk cartons to make planters. Fill each carton with soil. Collect one each of the following: scrap of aluminum foil, piece of string, piece of banana, tin can, plastic wrapper, green leaf. Bury one item in each milk carton planter. Keep the soil warm and damp. Once a week, over an 8-week period, have students unearth the items and record their appearance. At the end of the 8-week period, empty the containers and have students notice which items have decayed—these are the biodegradable ones.

- Have the class present a recycling show. Ask each student to make something different using milk cartons and then present the new use to the class or to the school during an assembly. Students could make toy buildings, planters, storage containers, and so on.

- Have students survey the items that are thrown away at home, using Activity Sheet 14: What's in The Trash? Follow up the survey with a class discussion in which students speculate about ways to reduce the amount of trash we discard daily.

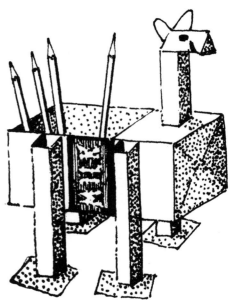

Additional Resources

Bailey, Donna. *What We Can Do about Recycling Garbage.* New York: Watts, 1991.

Simons, Robin. *Recyclopedia.* Boston: Houghton Mifflin, 1976.

Designing Recycling Posters

Overview

Students learn about the interaction of humans and their environment through a discussion of the importance of recycling. They then design posters to communicate the idea that recycling helps the environment.

Student Objectives

- discuss the ways in which several trash items can be recycled.

- design a poster to communicate the idea that recycling helps the environment.

Materials

- pencils

- sheets of white construction paper, approximately 18" x 24"

- colored felt-tip markers or crayons

Observing, Comparing, and Describing

1. Ask students to list all the kinds of things they throw away at home. Record these on the chalkboard. (For nonreaders, record ideas with simple line drawings.)

2. Ask students where garbage trucks take household trash. (*To landfills or incinerators*)

3. Speculate with students about what would happen if trash piled up inside the home for one year. What would the house look and smell like after one month? After six months? How would this change the way they live? (*It might make it difficult to move from room to room. There would be no place to sleep.*)

4. Write the word *interaction* on the board. Remind students that an interaction occurs when two or more things affect each other. Point out that an interaction occurs between people and their environment when we dispose of our trash.

5. Help students understand how household trash affects the environment. Land set aside for a garbage dump, for example, can no longer be a home for certain kinds of wildlife. Marshlands, which are home to ducks, geese, and other wildfowl, disappear when they are turned into landfill sites. Pollution from garbage sites can poison small streams and rivers, killing fish and other animals.

6. Write the word *recycle* on the board. Tell students that *recycle* means "to use again." Help students list the kinds of trash items that can be recycled.

note

The initial discussion and pencil drawing can be completed in one session. Adding detail and coloring to the poster will take one or two more sessions.

7. Ask students how they could encourage more people to recycle their trash. Allow time for sharing. Explain that graphic artists often communicate important ideas through posters. Tell the class that they will design posters to communicate the idea that recycling helps the environment.

Creating

1. Begin by asking students what kinds of things they could put in a picture to show that trash hurts the environment. List these on the chalkboard. Encourage students to be fanciful and inventive. ("You could draw a picture of a mountain of garbage 10 miles high!") Have students in small groups share ideas for pictures. Allow ample time for thinking and sharing.

2. Show students how to use pencil on the poster paper to draw an outline sketch of their ideas. Tell students to put in as much detail as possible with the pencil. The coloring can be done during a later session.

3. When students understand the procedure, distribute materials. Circulate, and offer assistance when needed. Encourage students to make their drawings as detailed and elaborate as possible, filling the entire sheet of paper. Older students might want to include a message on their poster, such as *Take Care of the Earth!* or *Recycle!*

4. In a later session, students can use felt-tip markers or crayons to color their posters. Help students cover the entire sheet of paper with color.

Evaluating

Display the finished posters. Have students notice and discuss the variety of ways in which their classmates communicated the idea that recycling helps the environment.

Final Touches

Display the posters around the school, or contact a local business, such as a bank, and arrange to have students' work displayed there.

Going Further

■ Arrange a field trip to a local recycling center.

■ Have students collect and recycle several kinds of items. Have students count and weigh the items they collect, and then graph them on a class chart. Use the proceeds from recycling aluminum cans to buy a special treat for the class.

Additional Resources

Bailey, Donna. *What We Can Do About Litter.* New York: Watts, 1991.

McQueen, Kelly, and David Fassler. *Let's Talk About Trash: The Kids' Book About Recycling.* Seattle: Waterfront Press, 1991.

Sisson, Edith A. "Conservation Awareness," in *Nature with Children of All Ages.* New York: Prentice-Hall, 1982.

Investigating Animal Camouflage

Overview

How does an animal's appearance help it hide from its enemies? What kinds of camouflage are most effective? Students begin the lesson by playing a game outdoors, "Toothpick Hide and Seek," in order to discover how color can serve as camouflage. Using scrap-paper collage, they create a background. They then create and "hide" several paper moths against the background.

Student Objectives

- observe that color and pattern can serve as camouflage to hide animals from their enemies.

- create a collage using scraps of magazines, newspaper, and tissue paper.

- use color and pattern to camouflage a paper moth.

Materials

- several boxes of wooden toothpicks in assorted colors, including green

- newspaper to cover work areas

- liquid starch or diluted white glue

- containers to hold the starch or glue, 1 per group of students

- stiff-bristle brushes, 1 per student

- old magazines and newspapers

- scraps of tissue paper in assorted colors

- scissors

- moth outlines, reproduced on construction paper, from Activity Sheet 15: Moth Outlines (page 140)

- magazines or library books showing pictures of butterflies and other insects

- construction paper, approximately 9" x 12"

Getting Ready

1. Scatter the colored toothpicks in a designated grassy area outdoors.

2. Cover work areas with newspaper.

3. Arrange starch or glue in containers. Place several brushes in each container.

4. Organize the following materials for distribution to groups of students: piles of paper scraps (containing bits of magazines, newspaper, and colored tissue paper), scissors, moth outline sheets, glue, and brushes.

5. Select a place in the room where finished collages can be set to dry undisturbed.

Observing, Comparing, and Describing

1. Ask students to name animals that eat insects. (*Birds, bats, small mammals, snakes, etc.*) Allow time for sharing.

2. Help students speculate about ways an insect, such as a moth or grasshopper, might hide from its enemies.

3. Tell students that they will be going outside to play a game called "Toothpick Hide and Seek." Show students a colored toothpick, and explain that the toothpick represents an insect. They (the students) are going to play the part of hungry animals. Their job will be to collect as many tasty insects as they can in three minutes.

4. Take students outdoors and show them the area of grass in which the "insects" are hidden. Teach them the signal you will use to begin and end the activity.

5. When students understand the procedure, have them begin collecting toothpicks. After three minutes (or less, depending on how many they have picked up), signal them to stop collecting, and have them return to class.

Drawing Conclusions

1. Help students draw conclusions about the effect of color on camouflage. The following questions are useful in guiding discussion:

How many toothpicks did you collect?

Did you pick up more of one color than of another color? How many more?

Which colors were the easiest to find? The hardest? Why?

2. Explain that insects and other animals often use color to blend in with their surroundings. A green grasshopper, for instance, would be much more difficult to find in the grass than a red one.

3. Show students magazine or library book pictures of various insects. Ask them to discuss how each insect uses color to *camouflage,* or hide, itself. Have students notice how patterns or splotches of color can help an insect blend in with a multicolored background. Students will notice that some insects, such as monarch butterflies, are very brightly colored. Point out that not every insect needs camouflage. The monarch feeds on poisonous milkweeds, which makes it distasteful to the birds that might try to eat it.

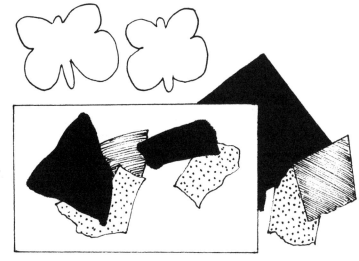

Creating

1. Tell students that they will create a multicolored background and camouflage a moth to hide in it.

2. Demonstrate the procedure:

Show students how to cut out two moths from Activity Sheet 15. Tell them to write their names on the back of each one. Set the two moths aside.

Pour some liquid starch or diluted glue onto a sheet of construction paper with a brush. Pick up a scrap of paper with the sticky brush, and put it down on the patch of glue. With more starch or glue, brush it flat against the paper.

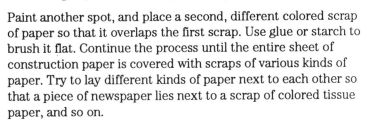

Paint another spot, and place a second, different colored scrap of paper so that it overlaps the first scrap. Use glue or starch to brush it flat. Continue the process until the entire sheet of construction paper is covered with scraps of various kinds of paper. Try to lay different kinds of paper next to each other so that a piece of newspaper lies next to a scrap of colored tissue paper, and so on.

When the background is finished, hold up one of the moths and ask students how you could disguise it so that it would really blend in with the background. Use liquid starch or glue to paste scraps of paper over the moth until it looks just like a piece of the background. Tell students that the second moth should be left blank—they will camouflage only one.

3. When students understand the procedure, distribute materials so that they can begin to work. Circulate, and offer assistance as needed.

4. Have students set their finished collages and moths in a designated area of the room to dry undisturbed.

Final Touches

1. When their moths and backgrounds are dry, show students how to slightly fold up the wings of the moths, as shown.

2. Have students select a place on their background to hide the camouflaged moth and another place for the plain moth. When students have chosen their places, help them glue the two moths to their backgrounds.

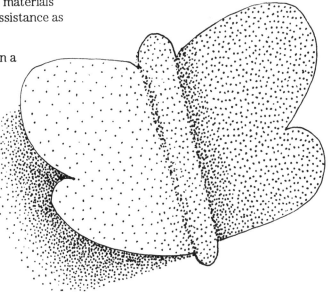

Evaluating

Display the dried collages. Have students notice how both color and pattern help camouflage the moths. Help them notice and discuss the contrast between the plain and the camouflaged moths.

Going Further

Have students create their own imaginary animals to hide outdoors. Ask students to draw, color, and cut out animals. Outdoors, let half the group place their animals where they will be concealed by camouflage. Have the other half of the group try to locate the camouflaged animals, and then have the groups switch roles.

Additional Resources

McDonnell, Janet. *Animal Camouflage:Hide & Seek Animals.* Elgin, Il: Child's World, 1990.

Tee-Van, Helen Damrosch. *Small Mammals Are Where You Find Them.* New York: Knopf, 1966.

Investigating Animal Adaptations

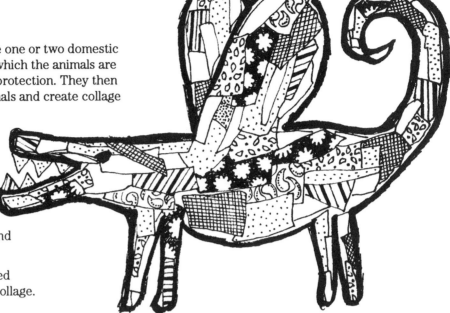

Overview

In this activity, students observe one or two domestic animals and notice the ways in which the animals are adapted for obtaining food and protection. They then invent their own imaginary animals and create collage pictures of them, using scraps of assorted papers and fabrics.

Student Objectives

- observe that animals have adapta tions that enable them to obtain food and protection from enemies.

- combine a painted or crayoned outline with paper or fabric collage.

Materials

- 1 or 2 live animals for students to observe in class, such as a pet cat, dog, bird, hamster, or rat.

- small portion of animal food

- various pieces of paper for collage, such as gift wrap, wallpaper sample pages, metallic paper, aluminum foil, tissue paper, construction paper–collection per group of students

- assorted scraps of fabric

- sharp scissors

- containers of water, 1 per student pair

- *either* black tempera paint in shallow containers and flat-bristle brushes, *or* black crayons

- newspaper

- masking tape

- colored construction paper, 18" x 24", 1 sheet per student

- stiff-bristle brushes

- containers of white glue

Getting Ready

1. Arrange to bring in one or two domestic animals for students to observe. One way to do this is to ask for volunteers to bring in their pets. If you are planning to bring in a cat or dog, make arrangements to have the animal taken home as soon as the lesson is over. Smaller animals should be brought in cages with sufficient food and drink to last the day. Be sure to allow time for the animal to become acclimated to the classroom before showing it to students.

2. Collect assorted kinds of paper and fabric. Students may bring these from home several days in advance of the lesson. Use sharp scissors to precut the fabric into small scraps no larger than 1" x 3".

3. Organize art materials for distribution during the lesson. Have containers of water and brushes ready for the practice painting outdoors.

4. Cover work areas with newspaper.

Observing, Comparing, and Describing

1. Tell students that every animal is *adapted,* or formed, for obtaining food. Humans have many *adaptations.* Our opposable thumbs enable us to grasp tools. To show how useful this adaptation is, ask several volunteers to come to the front of the class, and tape their thumbs to their hands with masking tape. Have them try to pick things up, to write on the chalkboard, and to tie their shoes or button their shirts.

2. Show students the animal and ask them to observe it very closely and to list the adaptations they see. The following questions are useful in guiding observation:

How are the animal's eyes adapted for seeing?

How else does the animal sense its environment?

If the animal has a tail, how does it use it?

How is the animal adapted for eating? (Offer the animal some food, and have students notice the way it eats.)

How is the animal's foot adapted for running, grasping, or hopping? (Have students notice the bottom of the foot as well.)

How is the animal adapted for hiding or escaping from its enemies?

note

You may want to divide this lesson into two sessions. In the first session, students can create outline shapes of their animals. In the second session, students can fill in the outlines with collage.

Creating

1. Help each student imagine an animal. Explain that their animal should have adaptations for defending itself against enemies and for getting food. Tell students that they can imagine either a real animal or one that no one has ever seen.

2. *If students are using tempera paint:* Take the students outdoors to an area of smooth pavement. Distribute containers of water and brushes, and have the class practice painting their animal shapes with water on the pavement. Encourage them to use large arm movements and to concentrate on painting the outlines only.

When students are ready, set a sheet of newspaper on the pavement before each of them, and place a sheet of construction paper on top of it. Replace the container of water with a container of black tempera paint. Have them paint features such as eyes, noses, ears, teeth, and claws, but leave the animal's torso blank. Encourage them to fill up as much of the construction paper as they can.

3. *If students are using crayon:* Have students practice drawing large animal outlines on sheets of newspaper. When they are ready, have them draw their animal shapes on construction paper. Ask them to thicken the outlines to at least 1/4 inch. Have them fill in such features as eyes, noses, ears, teeth, and claws, but leave the animal's torso blank. Encourage them to cover as much of the construction paper as they can.

4. Show students how to fill in the torso of their animal with collage. Use a stiff-bristle brush to cover the inside of the animal outline with glue. Next, select a variety of paper and/or fabric scraps to paste within the outline. Overlap pieces to cover the shape and to create the fur/scales/hide/hair of the imaginary animal. Cut small pieces of paper for eyes and other features.

5. When students understand the procedure, distribute materials, and let them begin. Circulate, and offer assistance as needed. Remind students to overlap pieces to cover the entire shape of their animal.

6. When students have finished, set the animals aside to dry undisturbed.

Evaluating

Display the finished animals. Have students notice and compare the different adaptations created by their peers. Allow students to talk about how their animal is adapted for survival.

Going Further

- Bring in pictures of different kinds of animals, and have students discuss the types of food each eats and whether each animal has a physical characteristic adapted for catching and eating the food. For instance, the long neck of a giraffe enables it to eat tree leaves.

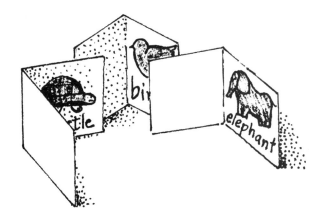

- Play a game in which students imitate animal behavior. Make a list of different kinds of animals. You will need enough animals for half of the class. Write the name of each animal twice, on separate pieces of paper. Place the pieces of paper in a can, and let each student draw a piece. The student silently reads the name of the animal (use magazine pictures or simple line drawings for nonreaders), returns the paper, and then imitates the animal in order to find a mate—the other student who drew a piece of paper with the same animal name.

Additional Resources

Barrett, Norman. *Birds of Prey.* New York: Watts, 1991.

Bender, Lionel. *Fish to Reptiles.* New York: Watts, 1988.

Lowery, Lawrence F. "Ecology," in *The Everyday Science Sourcebook.* Palo Alto, Calif.: Dale Seymour, 1985.

Investigating Seed Adaptations

Overview

How do seeds travel? In this fall activity, students go outdoors to collect different seeds for observation and classification. They notice that some seeds have become adapted to float through the air, while others fall to the ground or stick to animals. Then, using a variety of materials, they create their own imaginary seeds with adaptations for travel.

Student Objectives

- observe that seeds are adapted to disperse in a variety of ways.

- classify seeds according to whether they disperse by falling to the ground, sticking to animals, or floating through the air.

- use a variety of materials to sculpt an imaginary seed.

Materials

- newspaper to cover work areas

- bags or other small containers for carrying seeds, 1 per student

- *For kindergarten–grade 1:* large sheet of butcher paper and marker

- white glue and stiff-bristle brush

- *For grades 2–3:* Activity Sheet 16: Classifying Seeds (page 141)

- assorted materials for creating imaginary seeds: modeling clay, tape, toothpicks, string, paper clips, pipe cleaners, construction paper, bits of plastic foam, yarn, tissue paper, and so on.

- clear tape, 1 roll per group of students

Getting Ready

1. Cover work areas with newspaper.

2. Organize art materials for easy distribution to groups of students.

3. Select a weedy area outdoors for seed collection.

Observing, Comparing, and Describing

1. Have students share what they know about seeds. The following questions are useful in guiding discussion:

What is a seed? (*A plant part containing an embryo, capable of germination to produce a new plant*)

Where are seeds found? (*Inside fruits, on or near plants*)

> **SAFETY TIP**
>
> Be sure to check for students who might have respiratory difficulties or allergic reactions in weedy outdoor areas. You will need to make other arrangements for these students.

Why do plants have seeds? (*To reproduce*)

How are seeds different/similar? (*Size, shape, color, etc.*)

How do plants spread, or travel, to different areas? (*They fall or are picked up and carried by wind, water, or animals.*)

2. Help students understand that seeds are adapted, or formed, for travel. Without travel, seeds would fall directly under the parent plant. The area soon would become so overcrowded that the young plants could not survive.

3. Explain that some seeds, like those of the dandelion, float through the air. Others are hitchhikers, which travel by sticking to the fur of animals. Some fall to the ground, and others are carried by water.

4. Tell students that they will be going outdoors to collect as many different kinds of seeds as they can. They should look for seeds that float, fall, or stick. Many of the seeds on weeds are quite small and low to the ground, so the class will have to look very carefully to find them.

5. Distribute bags or other containers for collecting, and take students outdoors to collect seeds.

Classifying

For Kindergarten–Grade 1:

1. Gather students indoors in a circle on the floor around a large sheet of butcher paper. Use a marker to draw three circles on the butcher paper. Label the circles as follows: FLOAT, FALL, and STICK.

2. Ask students to remove the seeds from their bags and to sort them into three groups on the floor in front of them. In one pile, place seeds that *float* through the air, such as dandelion, milkweed, and thistle. In another pile, place seeds that *fall* to the ground. In a third pile, place seeds that *stick* to things, such as foxtail and cocklebur. (Students may find some of these on their socks!)

3. When students have sorted their seeds, use a stiff-bristle brush to cover the FLOAT circle with white glue. Have students come up individually to drop their floating seeds onto the sticky circle. Repeat the process with each of the other areas until all of the seeds have been glued to the sheet of butcher paper.

For Grades 2–3:

1. Bring students indoors, and have them sit at their desks or tables. Ask them to remove the seeds from their bags and to sort them into three groups. In one pile, place seeds that *float* through the air, such as dandelion, milkweed, and thistle. In another pile, place seeds that *fall* to the ground. In a third pile, place seeds that *stick* to things, such as foxtail and cocklebur. (Students may find some of these on their socks!)

2. Distribute Activity Sheet 16: Classifying Seeds. Show students how to use clear tape to attach seeds to the appropriate area of the worksheet.

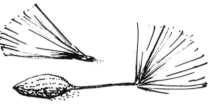

float

fall

stick

Drawing Conclusions

Have students examine the seeds after they have been classified. The following questions are useful in guiding discussion:

Are there more of one kind of seed than another?

How are the seeds that float similar or different? How does their structure help them to float?

How are the seeds that stick similar or different? How does their structure help them to stick?

How would you describe the seeds that fall to the ground?

What seeds don't seem to fit in any of these groups? How would you describe them?

Creating

1. Tell students that they will next create their own imaginary seed. Their seed must be adapted to travel in some way.

2. Demonstrate the procedure:

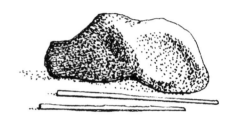

Shape a piece of modeling clay into a seed. Explain as you work that the class can make their seeds as large or as small as they like. Ask students to share ideas for possible seed shapes, such as long and narrow, round, or flat.

Show students a variety of materials, such as those listed in the "Materials" section at the beginning of the lesson. Explain that they will have to decide whether to make a seed that can float, stick, or fall to the ground. Help students generate ideas for ways to make a seed that can stick, float, or fall.

Explain that they should use as many types of materials as possible in order to make their seed look *unique,* or different, from anyone else's seed.

3. When students understand the procedure, distribute materials and have them begin. Circulate, and offer assistance as needed.

Evaluating

Display the finished sculptures. Have students compare and discuss the variety of ways their classmates created seeds that can float, fall, or stick.

Going Further

- Obtain mature blossoms of thistle and dandelion. Place them in the classroom so that students can observe them as they dry and go to seed. Have a volunteer blow on a dry dandelion head and observe how the seeds travel.

- Find branches of Scotch broom or other plants that still carry seed pods, and bring them to class. Let the branches dry. Have students observe the changes in the seed pods. Ask them to listen and watch for signs of seed dispersal. They can record their observations in a journal or logbook.

Additional Resources

Lowery, Lawrence F. "Ecology," in *The Everyday Science Sourcebook*. Palo Alto, Calif.: Dale Seymour, 1985.

Moncure, Jane B. *How Seeds Travel: Popguns & Parachutes*. Elgin, Il.: Child's World, 1990.

Overbeck, Cynthia. *How Seeds Travel*. Minneapolis: Lerner, 1982.

Creating Ecosystem Murals

Overview

Murals may be created in a variety of ways in the classroom. What follows is a description of several methods the teacher can use to guide students in the creation of a mural that depicts the plants and animals living in an ecosystem, whether it be the forest, ocean, desert, or prairie.

Student Objectives

- use a variety of materials to create a mural that depicts the interaction of plants and animals in an ecosystem.

- use a variety of media and design techniques in the creation of the mural.

Discusing

1. Have students review what they have learned about the ecosystem that the class has been studying. Ask them to share ways that the plants and animals in an ecosystem interact, or affect each other.

2. Tell students that they will be working to create a mural of their ecosystem. Explain that a *mural* is a large picture created on a wall.

3. Have students brainstorm a list of the plants and animals that should be included in their mural. Older students can work in groups to find plants and animals in resource books. Record their ideas on butcher paper.

Preparing the Mural Background

1. Obtain a roll or long section of colored butcher paper, sometimes called bulletin board paper. For an ocean mural, obtain blue paper; for the forest, obtain green; and so on. If you want your mural to show a background of field and sky, you can cut a length of blue and staple it along the top of the butcher paper.

2. If you have only white butcher paper available, have your students paint the background in a color appropriate to the ecosystem they are studying. Lay the paper over newspaper in an area of the classroom. Arrange containers of tempera paint and large-bristle brushes at intervals around the paper. Show students how to cover sections of the paper with long, broad, horizontal strokes. Have students come to the mural by turns to paint a small section of the background until the white has been completely covered.

3. Fasten the completed background to a section of the classroom wall.

Creating Plants for the Mural

note

Three different methods of creating plant forms are described below. Select the method that would be most rewarding for your students.

Method 1: Using Tempera Paint

In this activity, students mix tempera paints and use their new colors to paint sheets of paper. Later they cut them into large leaf shapes. Students observe that many variations of color can be made by adding black or white.

Materials

- newspaper to cover work areas

- 9" x 12" newsprint or construction paper, 1 per student

- stiff-bristle brushes for each color, 1 per student

- individual palettes for each student, such as aluminum pie tins or TV dinner trays

- tempera paint—2 pints yellow, 1 pint each blue, white, and black, poured into low, wide containers

- paper towels for wiping hands, several per group of students

Getting Ready

Cover the desks with newspaper. Distribute paper, brushes, and palettes.

Demonstrating the Procedure

First, use a brush to place a dab of yellow into a palette. Then dip some blue into the yellow, and stir the two colors together to make green. Next, dip some black or white paint into a corner of the palette. Mix the black or white with the green. Paint the resulting tint or shade all over half of the paper. On the other half of the paper, paint another mix of colors.

Tell students always to add the darker color to the lighter color. Explain that a *tint* is made by adding some color to white, and a *shade* is made by adding black to some color.

When students understand the procedure, distribute materials, and let them begin. After the paintings have dried, have the class cut out their finished leaf shapes. Staple their shapes to the mural to represent seaweed, tree leaves (use pieces of brown construction paper for the trunk), grass, and so on.

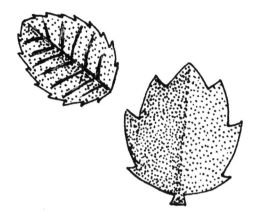

Method 2: Using Construction Paper

In this activity, students cut symmetrical leaf shapes from folded paper.

Materials

- many kinds of green paper, such as construction paper, gift wrap, and wallpaper

- scissors

- manila paper, 12" x 18"

- (optional) crayons or felt-tip pens

Getting Ready

Cut the green paper into rectangles of various sizes, allowing several pieces per student. Distribute the manila paper and scissors before the demonstration.

Demonstrating the Procedure

Use a large sheet of paper to demonstrate the process. Show students how to fold the paper in half, press down the fold, and cut the shape of half a leaf—long and thin, or short and broad. Open the paper, and have students notice the resulting shape. Help students speculate about how the edge could be varied—serrated, indented, and so on. Fold the paper again, recut the edge, and observe the new result.

When students understand the procedure, distribute the green paper, and let them begin. Students may use dark crayons or felt-tip pens to draw veins on their leaf shapes. Staple the finished leaves to the mural to represent seaweed, tree leaves, grass, and so on.

Method 3: Using Tissue-Paper Collage

In this activity, students overlay scraps of blue and yellow tissue paper to create green. They paste the scraps onto a leaf shape and cut it out when the paste has dried.

Materials

- newspaper to cover work areas

- black crayons

- sheets of white construction paper, 9" x 12"

- pie tins of liquid starch or diluted white glue

- stiff-bristle brushes

- many small pieces of tissue: blue, yellow, and green

- scissors

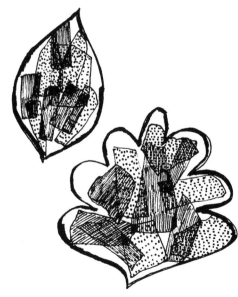

Getting Ready

Cover the work areas with newspaper. Organize the art materials for distribution during the activity.

Demonstrating the Procedure

Show students how to use a dark crayon to draw a large leaf shape on a piece of white construction paper. Explain that the leaf must be larger than their hand. Use your hand as a guide, and draw the leaf shape around it.

Spread some liquid starch or diluted glue onto the leaf shape with a brush. Pick up a piece of blue tissue with the sticky brush, and set it on the starch or glue. With more starch, brush it down. Pick up a piece of yellow, and set it down so that it overlaps the first. Have students notice the resulting green color. Continue to place bits of blue paper on the leaf and overlap them with yellow. Use shades of green tissue for variety. Cover the entire leaf shape.

When students understand the procedure, distribute the materials and have them begin. After the collages have dried, let students cut out their leaf shapes. They can use crayons or felt-tip pens to draw veins in the leaves if desired. Staple the finished leaves to the mural to represent seaweed, tree leaves (use strips of brown paper for the trunk), grass, and so on.

Creating Animals for the Mural

Method 1: Using Sponge Printing

In this activity, students use small pieces of sponge to stamp print color over an animal shape drawn with crayon.

note

Three different methods of creating animal forms are described below. Select the method that would be most rewarding for your students.

Materials

- newspaper to cover work areas

- crayons

- white or colored 9" x 12" and 18" x 24" construction paper

- palettes for printing, such as aluminum pie tins or TV dinner trays

- cellulose sponges cut into 1" or 2" rectangles

- spring-type clothespins as handles for sponge pieces

- tempera paint in assorted colors

- low containers for paint

- scissors

Getting Ready

Cover the work areas with newspaper. Organize the art materials for distribution during the activity.

Demonstrating the Procedure

Remind students of the kinds of animals that live in the ecosystem they have been studying. With a black crayon, draw a large animal shape on a piece of construction paper. Tell students that the animal must be larger than their hand. Place your hand on the construction paper to use as a guide, and draw the animal shape around it.

Use the crayon to add such features as eyes, nose, teeth, and fins.

Pour a tablespoonful of paint into a palette. Hold a sponge square with a clothespin. Dip it into the paint, wipe the excess off on the edge of the container, and print all over the animal. Do not cover the paper too thickly—allow some background color to show through.

After the paintings have dried, have students use scissors to cut out their animals. Have students discuss where various animals should be placed on the mural, and then staple the animals in the appropriate positions.

Method 2: Using Crayon-Resist

In this activity, students use crayons to draw a picture of an animal and then paint over the crayon drawing with a wash of tempera paint.

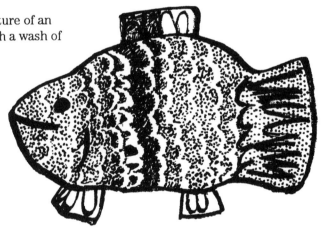

Materials

- newspaper to cover work areas

- tempera paint in assorted colors, diluted with water to the point that it resists wax crayon

- containers to hold the paint

- paintbrushes

- crayons

- construction paper, 9" x 12" or 18" x 24", 1 sheet per student

- scissors

Getting Ready

Set aside a table in the room at which students can paint over their crayon drawings. Cover the table with newspapers, and set containers of paint and brushes at intervals around the table.

Demonstrating the Procedure

Show students how to use crayons to draw a large animal shape on the construction paper. Explain that the animal must be larger than their hand. Use your hand as a guide, and draw the animal shape around it.

Press hard with the crayon to draw the features of the animal: eyes, nose, ears, fins, gills, and so on. Draw lines on the body of the animal representing fur, scales, patterns, and so on. Tell students to press hard with the crayon so that the tempera paint will resist the lines. When the drawing is complete, paint over the animal shape with tempera paint. Use broad strokes to cover the animal completely.

When students understand the procedure, distribute materials so that they can begin. After the paintings have dried, let students cut out their animal shapes. Have students discuss where various animals should be placed on the mural, and then staple the animals in the appropriate positions.

Method 3: Using Tagboard Bas-Relief

In this activity, students use small items such as toothpicks, straws, macaroni, and beans to create bas-relief sculptures of animals on a background of tagboard.

Materials

- newspaper to cover work areas

- scissors

- tagboard, 9" x 12" or 18" x 24", 1 sheet per student

- assorted small items to provide texture for the bas-relief, such as toothpicks, pieces of straws, macaroni, and beans, 1 collection per group of students

- containers of white glue, 1 per group of students

- stiff-bristle brushes, 1 per student

- soft brushes

- containers of tempera paint in assorted colors

Getting Ready

Organize the art materials for distribution during the lesson. Cover the work areas with newspaper.

Demonstrating the Procedure

Show students how to use pencil to draw a large animal shape on the tagboard. Explain that the animal must be larger than their hand. Use your hand as a guide, and draw the animal shape around it. Use scissors to cut out the shape.

Show students how to place bits of macaroni, straws, toothpicks, and beans over the animal shape to represent fur, scales, or to make patterns and designs. Tell students that when they have created a design they like, they should glue it into place.

Use a stiff brush to place thick blobs of glue on the tagboard. Set objects into the glue according to your design.

When students understand the procedure, distribute materials and let them begin. Finished bas-relief sculptures should be set aside in a safe place to dry.

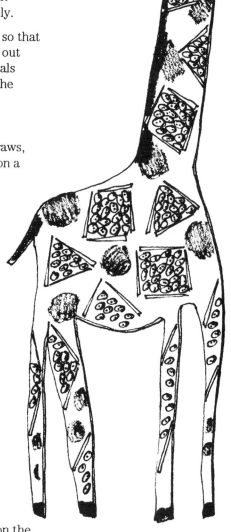

Show students how to use a soft brush and carefully paint over the dried bas-relief with tempera paint. After the painted sculptures have dried, let students decide where their animals should be placed on the mural. Staple the tagboard animals into position.

Evaluating

Have students observe and discuss the finished mural. The following questions are useful in guiding discussion:

How do the plants and animals interact in the mural?

What variation, or differences, can you find in the plants? In the animals?

Additional Resources

Alexander, Kay. "A Leafy Green Mural," in *Learning to Look and Create: The Spectra Program, Grade One.* Palo Alto, Calif.: Dale Seymour, 1987.

Energy

The Theme of Energy

The investigations in this section are organized around the theme of energy. In physics, *energy* is defined as "the ability to do work" or "the ability to make things move." In biology, energy provides living things with the ability to grow and to reproduce. Light, heat, sound, magnetism, and electricity are all manifestations of energy.

Artists use energy in its various forms to generate movement or intensity in a work of art. Some sculptural forms, such as mobiles, make use of wind or heat energy to maintain their motion. Neon and laser lights produce varied, brightly colored designs.

In the visual arts, *energy* often is expressed metaphorically. Students learn to evoke the quality of energy in their artwork. Bold lines, forceful brush strokes, and bright colors all contribute to vitality of expression in drawing and painting. By learning to evaluate the expressive qualities of their own work, students develop the ability to recognize the quality of energy in the work of other artists.

Introduction to Energy: Lines of Expression

Overview

This activity introduces students to the theme of energy. Students begin by discussing and role-playing the meaning of such phrases as, "I'm full of energy" or "I'm almost out of energy." A brain-storming session follows in which students identify various manifestations of energy, such as heat, light, electricity, magnetism, and wind. As artists, they then use crayon or charcoal to draw lines that express the quality of energy.

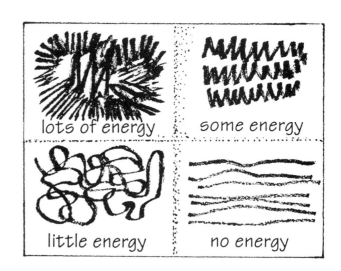

Student Objectives

- understand that energy is the ability to do work or to make things move or grow.

- identify the following manifestations of energy: heat, electricity, light, magnetism, and wind.

- use crayon or charcoal to draw lines that express varying degrees of energy.

Materials

- white drawing paper, 9" x 12"

- black crayons or charcoal

- If students use charcoal: newspaper; damp paper towels or rags for wiping hands

- (optional) Activity Sheet 17: Energy in My Home (page 142)

Getting Ready

1. For Kindergarten–Grade 1: Fold the sheets of drawing paper in half, and then open them up again to create two spaces for drawing.

2. If students will be using charcoal, cover work areas with newspaper, and organize damp paper towels or rags for distribution during cleanup.

Observing, Comparing, and Describing

1. Ask students whether they have ever heard someone say, "I'm full of energy!" The following questions are useful in guiding discussion:

What does this saying mean?

When do *you* feel this way?

What would someone full of energy look and sound like? How would the person walk, for instance? (Encourage volunteers to role-play this for the group.)

Extend the discussion by asking students similar questions about the saying, "I'm almost out of energy."

2. Write the word *energy* on the chalkboard. Tell students that energy is the ability to do work or to make things move or grow. Ask students to name various things that move or grow (plants, cars, people, and so on). Help students understand that everything that moves or grows uses energy.

3. Have students discuss the sources of energy. As the various sources are named, write them on the board. Include simple pictures for the benefit of nonreading or limited-English proficient students. The following questions are useful in guiding discussion:

Where do plants get their energy? (*From food nutrients and from light*)

Where do machines get the energy to move? (*From electricity, magnetism, light, etc.*)

Where do windmills get the energy to move? (*From the wind*)

Where do hot-air balloons get the energy to move? (*From heat*)

Where do people and other animals get their energy? (*The food we eat is converted to energy, such as the heat that warms our bodies.*)

Creating

1. Tell students that artists often try to show energy in their drawings, paintings, or sculptures. Explain that they will be using crayon or charcoal to draw lines that show various levels of energy.

2. Ask, "How could I draw a line that is full of energy?" (*Draw it quickly; use short, swift strokes or long, vigorous strokes; press hard with the crayon; etc.*) "How could I draw a line that has very little energy?" (*Draw it slowly, with long, loopy curves; press lightly; etc.*)

3. Tell students that when they make their drawings, they may want to use one line or many lines. They can fill a whole section with lines if that seems right. But there is one rule: They must not draw any pictures or use any symbols at all—no faces, cars, bolts of lightning, flowers, etc. The feeling of energy must come from the marks on the paper.

4. Have students pretend that they are holding a piece of crayon or charcoal in their hand. Guide them through a visualization of the drawing process.

Say, "Remember a time when you felt full of energy. Feel what that energy was like. Imagine you are feeling it again. Feel the energy come from deep inside, then into your arm, down into your hand, and into the crayon. Imagine that you are moving the crayon on the paper to let all that energy come out."

5. Demonstrate the procedure:

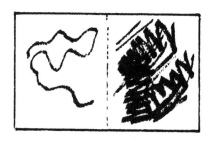

For Kindergarten–Grade 1: Show students a sheet of paper with a fold down the middle to create two areas for drawing. Explain that on one side of the fold they will draw lines that seem to be full of energy. On the other side they will draw lines that seem to have very little energy.

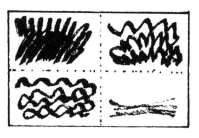

For Grades 2–3: Show students how to fold a paper twice and then open it up to create four areas for drawing. Explain that in one of the areas they should draw lines that seem to be full of energy. In the second area their lines should show a little less energy. In the third area their lines should show even less energy. In the last area their lines should hardly have any energy at all.

6. When students understand the procedure, distribute paper and crayons. As they work, circulate and offer assistance when needed.

Evaluating

Display the finished drawings. Ask students to compare the different kinds of marks their classmates used to show a high level of energy. Next, have them compare the marks that show a low level of energy. Help students notice both similarities and differences in the ways students expressed the various energy levels.

Going Further

- Have students look through old magazines to find pictures of various manifestations of energy. They may work in teams to cut and paste these into an energy collage.

- Younger students can work with their parents or guardians at home to complete Activity Sheet 17: Energy in My Home. At school, you can take students on a walk around the buildings and playground to observe and record things that move or grow. Older students may keep journals of energy sources they have noticed at school and home. Next to each item, have students indicate the energy source that produces the movement or growth.

- Show students slides or prints of abstract expressionist paintings. Ask them to compare the kinds of lines and brush strokes made by the artist. Have them discuss the level of energy expressed in the painting.

Additional Resources

Edwards, Betty. "Drawing Out Insight," in *Drawing on the Artist Within.* New York: Simon & Schuster, 1986.

Investigating the Sources of Light

Overview

Students learn about the sources of light energy by observing and comparing the light of a flashlight, lamp, and candle. In the art activity that follows, they create drawings of light sources, using chalk on black construction paper, which increases the intensity of the colors by contrast.

Student Objectives

- observe that light comes from a variety of sources and that the sun is the source of daylight.

- learn how to use chalk on a black background to accentuate the brightness of colors and to increase their intensity by contrast.

Materials

- black construction paper, 12" x 18", 1 sheet per student

- art chalk: white, yellow, red, orange

- small cups to hold chalk pieces

- damp cloths for cleanup

- large sheet of butcher paper

- masking tape

- a small collection of light sources—a flashlight, candle, small lamp, etc.

- sheet of white drawing paper, 12" x 18"

- spray fixative (you may use regular hair spray as a substitute if necessary)

- (optional) Activity Sheet 18: Lights in My Home (page 143)

Getting Ready

1. Set aside one sheet of black construction paper per student.

2. Soak the chalk pieces in water for one or two minutes before the lesson. This will cut down on the amount of dust produced while students are drawing.

3. Organize chalk by placing four or five pieces of one color (enough for a small group of students) into a small cup for easy distribution.

4. Have a damp cloth and paper towels available for each small group so that students can wipe their hands when finished.

5. Tape the large sheet of butcher paper to the wall or chalkboard to use for recording students' ideas during the opening discussion.

Observing, Comparing, and Describing

1. Ask students to share what they know about *energy*. List different kinds of energy (heat, electricity, sound, light, etc.). Define *energy* as "the ability to do work or to make things move or grow."

2. Explain that *light* is an important form of energy. Light from the sun provides solar energy to heat houses and to make things move, such as solar-powered engines. Light provides warmth, enables plants to make food, and helps us see the world around us.

3. Ask, "What kinds of things give light?" (*The sun, a lamp, candle, etc.*) "What gives light in your home? What gives light outdoors?" Record responses on the butcher paper. (Responses may be recorded as sketches for very young students.)

4. Show students such light sources as a flashlight, candle, and lamp. Light each one, and ask students whether the lights look the same or different. Ask, "Is one brighter than the other? Are the lights different colors?"

5. Have students look over the list they have brainstormed. Ask, "Are all these lights the same color? Are some lights brighter than others? Which light is the brightest?" Help students understand that the sun, the source of daylight, is the brightest light in our world.

6. Light a candle, and ask students to observe its light when the room is darkened. Ask, "When does this candle look brighter—when the room is light, or when the room is dark?"

7. Help students understand that all lights look brighter in darkness. Point out that it is the *contrast*, or difference of the dark background, that makes the candle's light appear brighter. The contrast increases the *intensity*, or brightness, of the color.

8. Demonstrate: Show the class a piece of white or yellow art chalk and two pieces of construction paper, one white and one black. Ask, "On which paper will this chalk look brighter?" Draw a few lines on each paper to show students how the black background makes the chalk appear brighter.

Creating

1. Distribute the paper and chalk. Suggest that students draw a scene of a street at night (with houses, cars, streetlights, stars, and so on). Have students experiment to discover which colors will contrast well with the black paper and look very bright.

2. Direct students to set their completed chalk drawings to one side so that you can spray them with fixative later (outdoors). Have students clean their hands and workplaces with the damp cloths and paper towels.

Drawing Conclusions

Bring the class together for a discussion of what has been learned. The following questions are useful in guiding discussion:

What sources of light have we learned about? (*Sun, fire, electric light, etc.*)

Which is the source of daylight? (*Sun*)

Why do lights look brighter when it is dark? (*Contrast*)

What are some of the different light sources we drew? (*Answers will vary.*)

Evaluating

Have students look at the completed drawings, and ask, "Which chalk colors look the brightest on the black paper? Which look the least bright?"

Going Further

You might ask students to find and record some of the light sources in their homes. Distribute Activity Sheet 18: Lights in My Home, and show students how to draw a light source in each of the boxes.

Additional Resources

Alexander, Kay. "The Harbor at Night," in *Learning to Look and Create: The Spectra Program, Grade Two*. Palo Alto, Calif.: Dale Seymour, 1989.

Lowery, Lawrence F. "Light," in *The Everyday Science Sourcebook*. Palo Alto, Calif.: Dale Seymour, 1985.

Describing and Classifying Colors

Overview

How does light energy enable us to see colors? How many shades of each color can we find? After exploring these questions in a group discussion, students investigate further by comparing the colors in magazine photographs and then cutting and pasting them into a collage.

blue

Student Objectives

- observe that light can be described, sequenced, and classified by such characteristics as color and intensity.

- observe that each color has many variations.

- select, cut out, and organize a variety of colored papers into a collage.

Materials

- *For kindergarten–grade 1:* sheet of butcher paper for each group of students; one 4" x 4" square of red, blue, green, brown, and yellow construction paper

- Activity Sheet 19: Color Page (page 144)

- paste

- old magazines and colored paper scraps

- scissors

- *For grades 2–3:* crayon for each pair of students: red, blue, green, brown, orange, or yellow

- damp paper towels for wiping hands and for cleanup

Getting Ready

1. For Kindergarten–Grade 1: Use large sheets of butcher paper rather than Activity Sheet 19: Color Page. Cut out a 4"x 4" square of red, blue, green, brown, and yellow construction paper. Paste one square in the middle of each sheet of butcher paper.

2. For Grades 2–3: Reproduce one copy of Activity Sheet 19: Color Page per student.

3. Put a small amount of paste on a scrap of paper for each student.

4. Have scissors and stacks of old magazines available for distribution.

Observing, Comparing, and Describing

1. Ask students to think of their favorite color. Allow time for sharing.

2. Help students understand that we see *color* because of light energy. When light strikes an object, some of the light is reflected back to our eyes. We perceive the reflected light as color. Without light, we would see no color at all.

3. Ask students to name some of the colors they see in the classroom. Note the many variations of each basic color. Ask, "How many different kinds of blue do you see?"

4. Have students wearing blue come up to the front of the class. Ask students to compare the different shades of blue they see. Ask, "Which blue is lightest? Which is darkest? Which is brightest, or more *intense*?"

5. Point out that *related colors* are like families; family members may look very much alike, but no two members look exactly the same.

Creating

1. For Kindergarten–Grade 1: Show students a sheet of butcher paper with a piece of colored construction paper pasted in the middle. Turn the pages of an old magazine to find a related color.

2. Show the class how to cut out the page and to trim it to show just that color.

3. Paste the color to the butcher paper next to the key color in the middle. Explain that students must find an assortment of related colors to paste on each piece of construction paper.

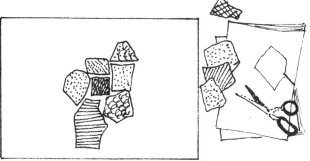

4. Demonstrate the proper procedure for using paste: Always spread the paste on the back of the smaller piece of paper, and then place the pasted piece on the larger piece or background. Be sure to use a small amount of paste.

5. Divide the class into color groups, distribute magazines and scissors, and help with the cutting. When one group has finished with a magazine, it may be passed to another group working on a different color.

6. Have students find and cut out a large pile of pieces before they begin to paste the pieces to the charts. Show students how to overlap colored pieces to cover the background.

7. For Grades 2–3: Follow the same procedure with Activity Sheet 19: Color Page. Begin by taking either a red, blue, green, brown, or yellow crayon to use as a key color. Show students how to color in the "key color" square in the middle of the page. Show how to cut and paste squares of related colors around the key color until the Color Page is filled.

Drawing Conclusions

Bring students together for a discussion of what they have learned. Ask, "Why is it harder to see colors at night than during the day?" (*There is less light at night.*)

Evaluating

Have each group or pair of students look over their chart or Color Page in order to find the lightest color variation, the darkest, and the brightest. Older students can count the number of color variations they found. Allow time for sharing.

Going Further

- Students can pursue their investigation of color families by making Color Books. For kindergarten and first-grade students, these may be made by stapling several sheets of construction paper together. Older students can use several copies of Activity Sheet 19 stapled together in a book. Students then can spend one period finding variations of red, the next finding blue, brown, yellow, and so on.

- In addition to using magazines, students can collect leaves and flower petals to show color variation. Scraps of paper or fabric brought from home can be added to the collection.

Additional Resources

Alexander, Kay. "Color Families," in *Learning to Look and Create: The Spectra Program, Kindergarten.* Palo Alto, Calif.: Dale Seymour, 1989.

Allington, Richard L. *Colors.* Milwaukee: Raintree, 1985.

Ardrey, Neil. *The Science Book of Color.* San Diego, Calif.: Harcourt Brace Jovanovich, 1991.

Investigating Light and Shadow

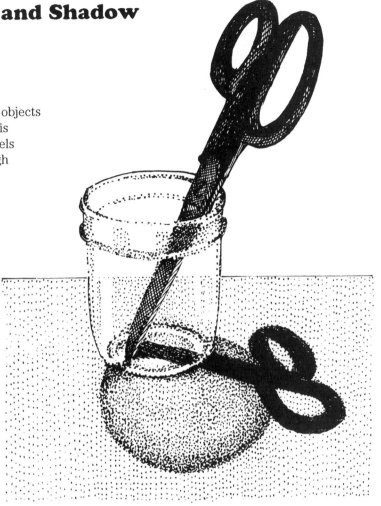

Overview

How are shadows made? Why do some objects cast darker shadows than others? In this lesson, students observe that light travels through some materials and not through others. Outdoors, students compare the shadows cast by a variety of objects. They then classify the objects according to whether they are opaque, translucent, or transparent.

Student Objectives

- observe that materials that block light cast shadows.

- compare materials and observe that light travels through some things and not through others.

Materials

- 2 large sheets of butcher paper

- masking tape

- marker

- a collection of various transparent, translucent, and opaque items to cast shadows, such as rulers, scissors, cans, kitchen utensils, plastic wrap, facial tissue, paper towels, plastic bags, glass and plastic bottles, jars, and leaves, placed in plastic tubs or other containers

- large sheets of white construction paper

- flashlight for demonstration

- (optional) Activity Sheet 20: Looking at Shadows (page145)

Getting Ready

1. Tape up a large sheet of butcher paper in the area where the opening discussion will be held. Use a marker to divide it into three columns with the following headings: "Dark Shadows," "Light Shadows," and "No Shadows." For the benefit of nonreaders, draw a black patch of color under the Dark Shadows heading and a blue patch under Light Shadows.

2. Place assorted transparent, translucent, and opaque objects into tubs or other containers for easy distribution. Have one tub by the butcher paper for demonstration during the discussion.

3. Tape a large sheet of butcher paper to the concrete or asphalt outside on the playground. Draw three large circles on the paper. Have the tubs of assorted objects and white construction paper nearby.

Observing, Comparing, and Describing

1. Ask students to list all the things they know about shadows. Allow time for sharing. Questions to prompt discussion include:

What causes a shadow? (*An object blocking light*)

When are there are no shadows? (*When there is no light*)

Are some shadows darker than others? (*Yes*)

When does a shadow move? (*When the object blocking light moves, or when the light source moves*)

2. Help students understand that objects that block light cast shadows. To demonstrate, shine a flashlight on the wall or chalkboard, and then have a volunteer stand between the light and the wall so that students can see the resulting shadow. Ask students to share other ways they can cast shadows (standing outside on a sunny day, holding an object up to a lamp, and so on).

3. Show students a collection of transparent, translucent, and opaque objects. Have them make predictions about which objects will cast dark shadows, which will cast light shadows, and which will cast no shadows. Record their predictions on the butcher paper.

4. Take the students outdoors and have them sit in a circle around you. Demonstrate how to hold each object over a sheet of white construction paper to observe its shadow.

5. Show students the tubs of assorted objects. Show them how to hold an object over a sheet of construction paper to observe its shadow. Students should notice whether the object casts a dark shadow, a light shadow, or no shadow at all.

6. Explain that after they have investigated an object, you will give a signal, at which time they should pass the object to the person on their right. Demonstrate and allow time for students to practice.

7. When students understand the procedure, distribute the objects and construction paper. Allow time for investigation. When each student has investigated four or five objects, ask students to set their objects on the ground in front of them.

8. Point out the three large circles on the butcher paper. Tell students that they will now group their objects according to whether they cast dark shadows, light shadows, or no shadows. Demonstrate by taking an opaque object, placing it in one of the circles, and saying, "This object casts a dark shadow, so it belongs in this circle." Demonstrate where to place a transparent or translucent object.

9. Have students come one by one to the butcher paper to place their objects in the appropriate circles.

Drawing Conclusions

1. Ask students whether they found any objects that cast no shadows at all. (The answer should be no.) Help them understand that all materials block light, though some let more light through than others.

2. Have students observe the objects that cast dark shadows. Ask them how these objects are different from objects that cast light shadows. Explain that light passes through *transparent* materials. Transparent materials, like clear glass or plastic, are easy to see through. Materials that let through some light, like a facial tissue, are called *translucent*. Materials they cannot see through at all, like a block of wood, a rock, or a book, block all light—these are called *opaque* materials.

Going Further

- Students in grades 2–3 may use Activity Sheet 20: Looking at Shadows to classify additional objects either at school or at home. Demonstrate how to write the name of the object (or draw a sketch of it) in the appropriate column.

- Have students record the movements of a shadow throughout the day. Let each student stand a small stick (a pencil or crayon will do) upright on a sheet of construction paper outdoors by setting its end in a small ball of modeling clay. Send students out every hour to trace the shadow.

  After several tracings, ask them to begin predicting where they think the shadow will be in the next hour by placing a mark on their sheet. Ask, "When is the shadow shortest? Longest?" Help students understand that the shadow moves as the earth rotates.

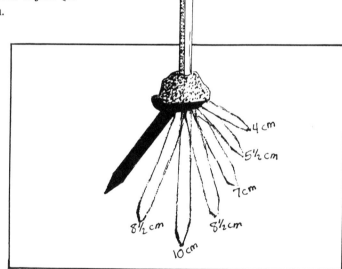

Additional Resources

Elementary Science Study: Light and Shadows. Hudson, N.H.: Delta Education, 1986.

"Me and My Shadow," in *Pieces and Patterns: A Patchwork in Math and Science, Project AIMS, Grades 5–9, Book #8.* Fresno, Calif.: Aims Education Foundation, 1986.

Drawing Shadows

Overview

How do artists draw shadows? In this outdoor activity, students observe and compare the color values of shadows cast by a variety of objects. Students then use shading techniques with crayon to reproduce the values on paper.

Student Objectives

- observe that shadows can be light or dark in color.

- use the technique of shading with crayons to change the value of colors.

Materials

- book, or other opaque object

- clear plastic cup, or other transparent object

- large sheet of white construction paper

- crayons, black and blue

- a collection of various transparent, translucent, and opaque items to cast shadows, such as rulers, scissors, cans, kitchen utensils, plastic wrap, facial tissue, paper towels, plastic bags, glass and plastic bottles, jars, and leaves, placed in plastic tubs or other containers.

- large sheets of white construction paper, 1 per student

Getting Ready

1. Place assorted transparent, translucent, and opaque objects into tubs or other containers.

2. Organize construction paper and crayons for easy distribution during the lesson.

Observing, Comparing, and Describing

1. Ask students to think of all the things they know about shadows. Allow time for sharing. Questions to prompt discussion include:

What causes a shadow? (*An object blocking light*)

What colors can shadows be? (*Almost any color, but usually gray, blue, purple, or black*)

What kinds of objects cast light shadows? (*Transparent or translucent objects*)

What kinds of objects cast dark shadows? (*Opaque objects*)

How does an artist draw a shadow? (*Using shading techniques*)

2. Take the students outdoors and have them sit in a circle around you. Hold up a transparent object, such as a clear plastic cup, and an opaque object, such as a book. Ask students what they notice about the difference in the shadows they cast. (The transparent object casts a light shadow; the opaque object casts a dark shadow.)

3. Explain that light passes through *transparent* materials. Transparent materials, like clear glass or plastic, are easy to see through. Materials that let through some light, like a facial tissue, are called *translucent.* Materials they cannot see through at all, like a block of wood, a rock, or a book, block all light—these are called *opaque* materials.

Creating

1. Tell students that they will be drawing pictures of light and dark shadows outdoors. Explain that they will learn how to use crayons to change the value of a color. Define *value* as "the lightness or darkness of a color."

2. Demonstrate the technique of shading:

To draw a very light shadow, move a blue crayon back and forth over white construction paper to cover an area approximately 3" x 3".

To draw a slightly darker shadow, draw a blue area just as you did before, and then *lightly* go over the blue with a black crayon.

To draw an even darker shadow, draw a blue area and then use a black crayon to cover the blue *heavily.*

Explain as you work that one always adds the darker color to the lighter color to make a shade. Discuss these colors with the class, using such terms as *blue, dark blue, midnight blue.*

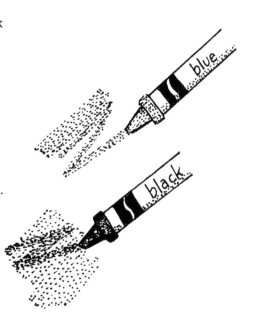

3. Stand a book on its end next to a clear plastic cup on a sheet of white paper. With a blue crayon, draw an outline of their shadows.

4. Use the blue crayon to fill in a light-blue shadow cast by the clear plastic cup. Use the blue and black crayons together to make a shade of blue for the darker shadow cast by the book.

5. Demonstrate how to make a line drawing of the object next to its shadow.

6. Distribute paper and assorted objects. Do not give out crayons at this time.

7. Ask students to begin by looking at the shadows cast by their objects. Have students group the objects by the value of shadow they cast: light, medium, and dark shadows. Circulate, and offer assistance when needed.

8. When students are ready, distribute the crayons so that they can draw pictures of the shadows and the objects.

Evaluating

1. Gather students together in the classroom when their drawings are finished. Display the drawings. Ask students to notice the shading techniques used by their classmates. Have them look at several drawings and identify places where students used black shading to alter the value of the colors.

2. Ask volunteers to share one thing they especially like about their own shadow drawing.

Going Further

- Create a "Light and Shadows" bulletin board with students' drawings. You can have students cut out their drawings and place them in three groups on the bulletin board, under "Transparent Objects," "Translucent Objects," and "Opaque Objects."

- Students can make shadow portraits by standing on a sheet of butcher paper and having classmates trace their shadows. The outlines can be filled in with tempera paint, allowed to dry, and cut out.

Additional Resources

Elementary Science Study: Light and Shadows. Hudson, N.H.: Delta Education, 1986.

"Me and My Shadow," in *Pieces and Patterns: A Patchwork in Math and Science, Project AIMS, Grades 5–9 Book #8*. Fresno, Calif.: Aims Education Foundation, 1986.

Investigating Hot and Cold

Overview

In this activity, students investigate the characteristics of hot and cold by feeling and describing different temperatures of water. They identify colors associated with cool temperatures and colors associated with warm temperatures. Using cool or warm colors of tissue paper, they then create a mixed-media collage.

Student Objectives

- observe that heat has identifiable characteristics.

- observe that some colors can seem cool and others can seem warm because of their associations.

- use cool or warm colors of tissue paper and dark-colored felt-tip pens (or black tempera paint) to create a mixed-media picture.

Materials

- assorted small pieces of tissue paper, approximately 2" x 3" to 3" x 4", some in warm colors (yellow, orange, red) and others in cool colors (blue, turquoise, violet, some greens)

- containers to hold the tissue paper, such as shoe boxes, trays, or aluminum pie tins

- newspaper to cover work areas

- wide and narrow felt-tip pens in dark colors, *or* small brushes and black tempera paint

- stiff-bristle brushes, 1/2" wide, 1 per student

- large sheets of white construction paper, 12" x 18", 1 per student

- aluminum pie tins of liquid starch or diluted white glue, 1 per group of 4 students

- containers to hold water, 3 per group of 4 students

- cold, lukewarm, and hot water source

- paper towels

Getting Ready

1. Cut or tear many small pieces of tissue paper. Pile the warm colors in containers for easy distribution. Do the same for the cool colors. Prepare one container of either warm or cool colors for every group of four students. Half of the groups will have a container of cool colors to work with, and the other half will have a container of warm colors.

2. Cover work areas with newspaper.

3. Organize brushes, white paper, and the liquid starch or glue for easy distribution during the lesson. Have felt-tip pens or small brushes and tempera paint ready for the second part of the lesson.

4. Just prior to the lesson, prepare three bowls or containers of water for each group of four students; one containing water that is about as hot as a student's hand can stand, one with lukewarm water, and one with cold water. Place the containers containing lukewarm water on tables where groups of students will investigate.

5. Place several paper towels at each table.

Observing, Comparing, and Describing

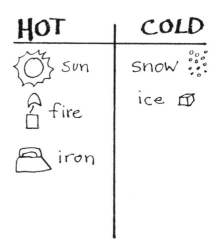

1. Ask students to list things that are warm or hot. Write the word *hot* on the chalkboard, and record their ideas. Next, have them list things that are cool or cold, and record these ideas as well. (For nonreaders, record their ideas in the form of simple line drawings.)

2. Point out the containers of water at each table. Tell students that when you give a signal, they should place their fingertips in the water and observe how the water feels. Give the signal, and have students keep their fingertips in the water as you ask questions to guide their observations:

How does the water feel? Is it hot, cold, or somewhere in between— warm or lukewarm or cool?

Name some other things that might feel this hot or cold.

3. Distribute the containers of hot water. Have students carefully place their fingertips in the hot water and observe how it feels, and then place them in the lukewarm water. Let them describe the sensation. (The lukewarm water will now feel cold.)

4. Distribute the containers of cold water. Have students place their fingertips in the cold water and observe how it feels. Next, have them remove their fingertips from the cold water and place them in the lukewarm water. Let them describe the sensation. (The lukewarm water will now feel warm.)

Drawing Conclusions

1. Speculate with students about why the lukewarm water felt warm after the cold water, and why it felt cold after the hot water.

2. Tell students that *temperature* is the amount of hotness or coldness of a thing. Help students realize that telling temperature by the sense of touch is relative and not accurate. For instance, it may seem hot in the classroom, but after being outdoors on a hot, sunny day, the classroom will seem cool.

Observing, Comparing, and Describing

1. Explain that we often think of hotness or coldness when we see certain colors. Ask students to look around the room and to identify colors that seem to be cold or cool. Questions to guide discussion include:

What color makes you think of ice? (*Probably white or light blue*)

What color makes you think of cold shadows? (*Probably blue or purple*)

What color makes you think of cold water? (*Probably blue or blue-green*)

2. Have students find colors in the room that seem to be warm or hot. Questions to guide discussion include:

What color makes you think of the hot sun? (*Probably yellow*)

What color makes you think of fire? (*Probably orange or yellow*)

What color makes you think of a fever? (*Probably red or orange*)

3. Help students understand that although a blue object is not necessarily colder in temperature than a red one, the color blue often reminds us of cold things. Artists often use shades of blue to create pictures that express cold, and shades of yellow or red to create pictures that express warmth or heat.

Creating

1. Tell students that they will create a tissue-paper collage using either warm or cool colors. Demonstrate how to make the collage:

Use either warm or cool colors; don't mix them. First, with a brush, spread some liquid starch or diluted glue onto a small area of the white paper.

Using the sticky brush as a tool, pick up any *dark* color from the pile of tissue paper, and place it on the prepared area. With more starch, brush it down.

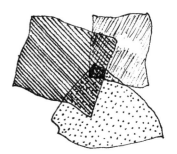

Paint another area of the white paper with glue. Pick up another, lighter, different-sized piece of tissue, and place it down on the second area so that it overlaps the first scrap. Always place lighter colors on top to let darker colors show through. Have students notice the color that results from overlapping the pieces of tissue.

2. Ask students to choose one set of colors to make either hot or cold pictures. Designate certain tables or areas as "hot" or "cold" tables, and have students sit at the appropriate places.

3. Distribute the containers of tissue paper, brushes, white construction paper, and liquid starch or diluted glue.

4. Circulate, and offer assistance as students begin to work. Encourage students to cover the entire sheet of white paper with pieces of overlapping tissue.

5. When students have finished, set aside the collages to dry overnight.

Final Touches

Distribute dark-colored felt-tip pens, or small brushes and containers of black tempera paint. Have students draw outline pictures of hot or cold subjects on their collages, depending on whether they used hot or cold colors.

Evaluating

Display the finished collages. Have students notice the subjects students chose and their relation to warm or cool temperatures.

Going Further

- Have students investigate different kinds of thermometers. Bring various kinds to class, such as mercury, alcohol, and digital. Have students notice that when they touch a thermometer, the heat of their hands will change the temperature reading. Ask students to touch the thermometer with an ice cube and observe what happens.

- Older students can measure temperatures around the school. Help students use graph paper to prepare a map of the school grounds, including the location of buildings, trees, playground equipment, and so on. Have them use sturdy metal thermometers to measure the temperatures of the air and soil in different locations around the grounds. Students can write the temperatures in the appropriate squares on the map.

Additional Resources

Alexander, Kay. "Hot and Cold," in *Learning to Look and Create: The Spectra Program, Grade One.* Palo Alto, Calif.: Dale Seymour, 1987.

Olesky, Walter. *Experiments With Heat.* Elgin, Il.: Childrens, 1986.

Using Heat Energy to Melt Ice Cubes

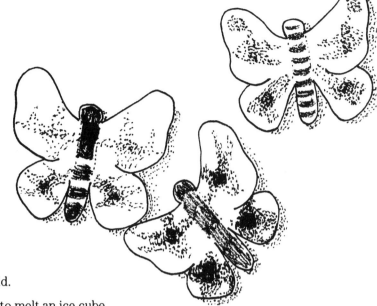

Overview

These outdoor investigations of heat energy begin with an exciting race. Students work in teams to be the first to melt an ice cube. Then, using chunks of ice and liquid tempera paint on colored construction paper, students create free-flowing designs that later can be cut out in the shape of butterflies.

Student Objectives

- observe that adding heat can cause matter to change from a solid to a liquid.

- use cooperative problem-solving skills to melt an ice cube.

- use ice and liquid tempera paint to create free-flowing designs on colored construction paper.

Materials

- 1 small ice cube per group of 4 students

- containers to hold the ice cubes, such as cut-off milk cartons or small aluminum pie tins

- brushes

- liquid tempera paints in assorted colors

- containers to hold the paints

- Activity Sheet 21: Butterfly Outline (page 146) reproduced on brightly colored construction paper, approximately 9" x 12", 1 per student

- newspaper

- masking tape

- 1/2 cupful of crushed ice, or 4 ice cubes per student

- crayons or markers

- scissors

- (optional) Activity Sheet 22: Things That Melt (page 147)

Getting Ready

1. Fill an ice cube tray 1/2 full so that the resulting ice cubes will be half the usual size. Freeze.

2. Select areas outdoors where the ice cube race can be held and where papers can be taped down on the asphalt or concrete for the painting activity.

3. Place several brushes into each container of tempera paint. Organize tempera paints, brushes, and butterfly outlines for easy distribution during the art lesson, which should take place outdoors on an asphalt or concrete surface.

Observing, Comparing, and Describing

1. Show students the ice cubes. Begin by asking the class to share what they already know about solids, liquids, and heat. The following questions are useful in guiding discussion:

What is an ice cube made of? (*Water*)

Why is it solid right now? (*It is frozen.*)

How else can water appear? (*As a liquid or gas*)

What could cause this ice cube to change from a solid to a liquid? (*Adding heat*)

What kinds of things could produce heat to melt this ice cube? (*Hands, the sun, candle flame, etc.*)

2. Tell students that the class is going to have a race. They will be working in teams of four outdoors. Each team will be given an ice cube in a container. Their task will be to try to find a way to make their ice cube melt faster than any other team's cube.

Explain the rules:

The ice cubes cannot be broken, eaten, or placed in anyone's mouth.

Each ice cube must stay in its container until it is melted.

3. When students understand the directions, distribute the ice cubes, and let the teams begin. Circulate, and offer assistance when needed. You might offer hints, such as:

Which materials on the playground are warmer than others? Can you find a warm surface on which to set the container? (*Dark-colored materials; metal objects, etc.*)

How can you use body heat to help melt the cube without removing it from the container? (*Hold the container in both hands; breathe on the cube, etc.*)

note

If the weather does not permit outdoor activities, both the ice cube race and the ice cube paintings can be done indoors.

note

The ice cube paintings take from 30 minutes to an hour to melt. Students will enjoy checking on the progress of their paintings, but the teacher should plan another activity to occupy the class during the melting period. Students might write a story entitled "If I Were an Ice Cube..." or draw a series of pictures to illustrate different ways to melt an ice cube.

note to kindergarten–grade 1 teachers

In some classrooms this activity is more successful when students work in pairs rather than in groups of four.

Drawing Conclusions

1. Have students from each group share their strategies for melting the ice cube. Point out that every group was successful in melting its cube, although some cubes melted more quickly than others.

2. Explain that *heat* is a form of energy. Remind students that energy is the ability to do work or to make things move or grow. Heat causes tiny particles in the ice, called molecules, to move about more quickly. As these particles move, they break apart, and the water changes from a solid to a liquid state.

Creating

1. Have students sit in a semicircle outdoors where they easily can see and hear your directions. Show students how to use melting ice to create a painting.

Place a sheet of construction paper printed with the butterfly outline on a piece of newspaper. Use masking tape to fasten the corners of the newspaper to the ground.

Dip a brush into a container of liquid tempera paint. Wipe the excess paint against the edge of the container. Dab a thick spot of paint in the center of one of the butterfly wings. Do the same in the center of another wing. Using a different color, place a spot in the center of each of the remaining wings.

Next, place an ice cube directly on top of each spot of tempera paint. If you are using crushed ice, place a small pile of ice (about 2 teaspoons) on top of each spot.

2. Explain that it will take some time for the ice cube to melt. As it melts and flows, the water will move the paint across the paper to create a free-flowing design.

3. When students understand the procedure, distribute materials, and let them begin.

4. When students are finished, have them begin another activity (see note next to "Observing, Comparing, and Describing," page 114). From time to time, allow students to check on the progress of their ice cube paintings.

Evaluating

When the ice cubes have melted completely, allow students to walk around and look at the resulting paintings. Have them notice how the melting ice moved the paint across the paper, in some cases mixing colors together.

Final Touches

1. Show students how to pick up their paper, quickly tilt it so that the excess water runs off to one side, and set it down again. Demonstrate how to fold the paper in half along the body of the butterfly so that the two painted sides are facing each other. Use the flat of your hand to press the folded paper. Open the paper, and have students notice the symmetrical pattern that has been created. Lay the paper flat to dry.

2. Later, when the paintings are completely dry, have students use crayons or markers to color the bodies of the butterflies. They can then use scissors to cut out the butterfly shapes. These make an attractive display when arranged on a bulletin board with tacks or pins through the bodies and the wings slightly folded away from the wall.

Going Further

■ Have students identify materials at home that can be melted. They can record their findings on Activity Sheet 22: Things That Melt.

■ Students can create lovely colored windows with melted crayon pieces. In small groups, under adult supervision, have students use potato peelers to make shavings from old, discarded crayons. Next, have students arrange the shavings on a sheet of waxed paper. Cover the paper and shavings with another sheet of waxed paper, placing the waxed side down. The sheets of waxed paper containing the crayon shavings should then be placed between several sheets of newspaper. Have an adult iron the newspaper to melt the crayon shavings. The resulting colored window can be framed with strips of black construction paper and hung in the room where sunlight will shine through it.

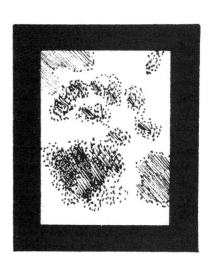

Additional Resources

Lowery, Lawrence F. "Heat," in *The Everyday Science Sourcebook*. Palo Alto, Calif.: Dale Seymour, 1985.

Painting the Ocean Currents

Overview

What are ocean currents? What causes the currents to move? In this activity, students observe that heat energy can create a current in water. They observe that a current can move in a circle or in waves or in a fairly straight line. Next, students use cardboard combs and tempera paint to create linear designs depicting imaginary ocean currents.

Student Objectives

- observe that heat can be a source of ocean currents.
- create pictures of ocean currents by using cardboard combs to make linear designs in wet paint.

Materials

- hot plate
- transparent coffee pot
- large, clear jar
- blue liquid food coloring, 1 small container
- dropper
- powdered tempera in assorted colors: light blue, light green, dark blue, dark green, purple, and white
- shallow containers to hold the paint mixture, such as aluminum pie tins
- liquid starch or dishwashing liquid
- stiff cardboard, enough for a 2" x 3" piece per student
- scissors
- newspaper to cover work areas
- 1" brushes, 1 per student
- white construction paper or tagboard, approximately 9" x 12"
- paper towels

Getting Ready

1. Set the hot plate on a sturdy table where students can see it easily. (Do *not* turn on the hot plate at this point.) Fill a transparent coffee pot with cold water and set it carefully on the hot plate so that the bottom of the pot rests on only one side of the heating element. Fill a large, clear jar with water, and place it on the table next to the hot plate. Set a container of blue food coloring nearby.

2. Place 2–3 tablespoons of powdered tempera paint in each shallow container. Add enough liquid starch or dishwashing liquid to create a thick mixture with the consistency of glue. For each group of four students, prepare three containers of color, one of which contains light blue.

3. To make combs, cut cardboard into 2" x 3" pieces. Cut a series of unevenly spaced notches into the long edge of each.

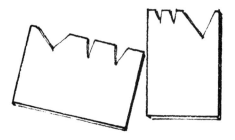

4. Set aside an area of the room where the finished paintings can dry undisturbed.

5. Cover work areas with newspaper.

6. Organize art materials for easy distribution during the lesson.

Observing, Comparing, and Describing

1. Have students share what they know about oceans. The following questions are useful in guiding discussion:

What is an ocean? (*Large body of salt water*)

What animals live in the ocean? (*Fish, whales, clams, lobsters, jellyfish, etc.*)

How do people use the oceans? (*Transportation, fishing, recreation, etc.*)

What causes the water in the oceans to move? (*Winds, ocean currents, earthquakes, etc.*)

2. Tell students that the oceans contain currents. A *current* is like an underwater stream or river that flows through an ocean. Ocean currents carry important nutrients from the bottom to the surface of the water, where fish can feed on them. Currents move certain animals, like jellyfish, from one place to another. It is thought that whales swim in ocean currents as they migrate during the year.

3. Tell students that they are going to try to make a current in the classroom. Show students the clear glass jar of cold water. Ask students to predict what will happen when you add several drops of food coloring to the surface. What will happen to the water? To the food coloring?

4. As you add the food coloring to the cold water, ask students to observe and discuss what they see. The following questions are useful in guiding discussion:

What happened to the color? (*It settled on the bottom of the jar.*)

What movement, or current, do you see in the water? (*Very little observable movement*)

5. Remind students that a current is like an underwater stream that moves through water. Explain that since the water shows no movement, no current exists in the jar.

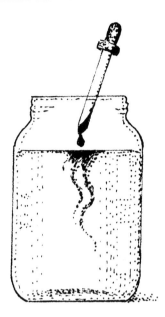

6. Show students the hot plate and clear coffee pot. Ask students to predict what will happen when you add several drops of food coloring to the water and then turn on the hot plate.

7. Add coloring to the water, and turn on the heat. Ask students to observe and discuss what they see. The color will first drop down into the water. As one side of the water becomes heated, students will see a definite current in the water. Ask them to describe the movement of the current through the water. (It will move in a fairly straight line or in small waves, then flow in a large circle through the water.) Turn off the hot plate and dispose of the hot water safely.

Drawing Conclusions

1. Have students discuss the difference between the movement of the food coloring in the cold water and heated water.

2. Write the word *energy* on the chalkboard. Remind students that *energy* is the ability to do work or to make things move or grow. Explain that heat energy caused a current to move through the water. Heat energy causes some of the currents in an ocean to move. Some currents in the ocean are caused by other forms of energy, such as wind.

3. Ask, "How is an ocean heated? Where does the heat come from?" Help students understand that an ocean is heated mostly on the surface, by the sun, though heat can rise also from the bottom, from undersea volcanoes, hot springs, or fissures.

Creating

1. Tell students they next will create pictures of imaginary ocean currents. Display several of the cardboard combs, and explain that they can be used to make line designs over a painted background.

2. Show students how to paint the background. Dip a large brush into the light-blue or light-green paint, and wipe excess paint against the side of the container. Using long, horizontal brush strokes, cover the surface of a large sheet of construction paper.

3. Dip the notched edge of a comb into a darker color, such as dark blue or purple. Drag the comb across the paint surface to make a curve, zigzag, or series of waves. Show students how to wipe the excess paint from the comb with paper towel before dipping it back into the paint.

4. When students understand the procedure, distribute the painting materials, and have them begin. Circulate, and offer assistance when needed.

Evaluating

Display the finished designs. Have students notice and compare the different kinds of lines made by their classmates: straight, curving, zigzag, or waving.

Going Further

- Students can observe a water current caused by wind. Use a piece of cardboard to fan air across the surface of a long, wide container of water. Sprinkle some sawdust onto the water, and students will see that the water moves in a large, circulating path. Explain that winds are the most important causes of ocean currents. Older students can research wind and ocean currents in an encyclopedia or other reference book.

- Students can observe a water current caused by salinity. Give each group of students two clear containers, one filled with plain water and the other filled with salt water. Have students add a drop of dark food coloring to each container and observe the results. Students will notice that the food coloring in the saline solution mixes much more rapidly than the coloring in the plain water. Explain that in a similar way, salinity causes parts of the ocean to move in currents.

Additional Resources

Agler, Leigh. *Liquid Explorations*. Berkeley, Calif.: Lawrence Hall of Science, University of California, 1987.

Alexander, Kay. "Cardboard Comb Designs," in *Learning to Look and Create: The Spectra Program, Grade Two*. Palo Alto, Calif.: Dale Seymour, 1987.

Investigating Magnetism

Overview

What kinds of objects are attracted to a magnet? Students discover the answer to this question by examining, predicting, testing, and classifying a variety of magnetic and nonmagnetic objects. They then work with clay to create small, textured plaques that can be used to decorate magnet holders.

Student Objectives

- describe and classify materials according to whether they are magnetic or nonmagnetic.

- create texture plaques to decorate magnets.

Materials

- assorted small objects made of various materials, such as small screws, bolts, bits of wood, clay, tinfoil, pebbles, cotton balls, staples, and pennies

- small paper bags, 1 per group of students

- small bar magnets, 1 per student

- length of wire for cutting clay

- 25-lb bag of buff ceramic clay for 25–30 students

- large plastic bag

- (optional) butcher paper

- Activity Sheet 23: Classifying Magnetic Objects (page 148), 1 per group of 4 students

- individual place mats for working with clay, such as pieces of vinyl or oilcloth or fabric-backed wallpaper samples

- assorted gadgets and natural objects for impressing and scratching the clay

- white glue

Getting Ready

1. Collect a variety of small objects for students to test with magnets. Distribute these into small paper bags so that each group of four students will have a bag of objects to investigate.

2. Obtain small bar magnets from a local hardware store. Look for the kind that are commonly used on refrigerators.

3. Use a length of thin wire to cut sections of clay. For each student, roll a section into a ball the size of an egg. Seal the clay eggs in a large plastic bag so that they will not dry out before the lesson.

4. Organize science and art materials for easy distribution during the lesson.

Observing, Comparing, and Describing

1. Begin by asking students to share what they know about magnets. Record their ideas on butcher paper or on the chalkboard. The following questions are useful in guiding discussion:

What is a magnet? (*A lodestone or mass of iron, steel, or alloy that attracts iron or steel*)

What does a magnet look like? (*Any shape*)

What does a magnet do? How is it used? (*Attracts iron or steel; used in compasses, to hold notes to refrigerators, to hold cabinet doors closed, etc.*)

What kinds of things will stick to a magnet? (*Objects of iron or steel*)

2. Show students a paper bag containing a variety of objects. Explain that an object that is attracted to a magnet is called *magnetic*. An object that is not attracted is called *nonmagnetic*.

3. Show students Activity Sheet 23: Classifying Magnetic Objects. Point out the two areas on the activity sheet, one for magnetic materials and one for nonmagnetic materials. Tell students that they will be working in groups of four to predict whether the objects in the bag will be magnetic or nonmagnetic. If they think an object is magnetic, they should place it in the appropriate area on the activity sheet. Model this for the class by holding up an object, having students predict, and placing it in the appropriate area on the activity sheet. Repeat several times until students understand the procedure.

4. Give each group of four students a bag of objects and an activity sheet. Have the groups examine the objects, predict whether they are magnetic or nonmagnetic, and place them in the appropriate area on the activity sheet. Circulate, and offer assistance when needed.

5. When students have finished placing the objects on the activity sheets, explain that they will next use magnets to test each object. The following rule will help students work cooperatively:

Students in a group must take turns testing each object. For example, if the first student tests an object and finds that it is magnetic, he or she must pass it to the next person to test. When the second person has tested the object, he or she must pass it to the third, and so on. When all agree that the object is magnetic, they should place it in the appropriate space on the activity sheet.

6. When students understand the procedure, distribute the magnets, and allow them to begin. Circulate, and offer assistance when needed.

7. When students have classified their objects, collect the magnets.

note

Students should be organized into groups of four for the lesson.

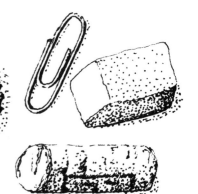

Drawing Conclusions

1. Have each group share their classification scheme. Ask students whether they were surprised by any of the results.

2. Explain that magnets are attracted to metal that contains iron or steel. Ask students whether refrigerator doors contain iron or steel. (*Yes, since magnets are attracted to refrigerator doors. Many people use small magnet holders to keep notes and pictures in place on their refrigerators.*)

Creating

1. Tell students that they will be creating their own magnet holders out of clay.

2. Place a ball of clay in the center of a place mat. Flatten and smooth the ball with the palm of your hand to create a circle approximately 3/8" thick and 2" in diameter.

3. Explain that *texture* is the way something feels, whether it is rough, smooth, bumpy, prickly, and so on. Show students a variety of objects, and ask them what kinds of textural effects some of the objects might make when pressed into the clay. Ask students what kinds of textures their own fingers, knuckles, and palms might make.

4. Make textures using only your hands, by poking, pinching, squeezing, scratching, and so on with your fingers, knuckles, and palms. Have students notice and discuss the results.

5. Experiment with the effects of pressing each of several objects into the clay.

6. Distribute clay, mats, and an assortment of objects to each group of students. Circulate, and offer assistance as students work. Help students experiment to create regular and repeat patterns. Before the clay becomes too dry, have students create a final plaque, scratch their initials on the back, and place the plaques on a shelf to dry.

Evaluating

Display the dried plaques on a table where students can walk around and see them. Guide students to observe the variety of textures created by their classmates. Call on individuals to tell how they created textural effects.

Final Touches

1. Dry the plaques for at least a week before firing.

2. After the plaques have been fired, glue a small bar magnet to the back of each to create a decorated magnet.

Going Further

- Students can investigate the force of magnetic fields. Have students work in pairs to push the ends of two bar magnets together in various ways. They will feel the force of attraction or repulsion between the two magnets. Have them also test the middle and sides of the magnets. Explain that what they feel are the magnetic fields surrounding the magnets.

- Have students investigate to discover whether a magnetic field can pass through glass, plastic, or paper. Give students glass and plastic jars, index cards, magnets, and pieces of steel or iron. Have them discover whether a magnet held against the outside of the jar can attract a piece of metal on the inside. The experiment can be repeated with a plastic glass. Let students discover whether a magnet will attract an iron object through an index card.

Additional Resources

Alexander, Kay. "Texture Plaques," in *Learning to Look and Create: The Spectra Program, Grade One.* Palo Alto, Calif.: Dale Seymour, 1987.

Strongin, Herb. *Science on a Shoestring.* Menlo Park, Calif.: Addison-Wesley, 1991.

Activity Sheet Blackline Masters

Activity Sheet 1

Solids in My Home

Find four solid things in your home.
Draw a picture of one thing in each box.

LESSON 3

Activity Sheet 2

Looking at Grains of Sand

1. How many different kinds of sand grains can you find? _____

2. Draw the different shapes you found:

3. List the different colors:

_____

_____

_____

4. Make a row with grains of sand, like this:

About how many grains make a row as long as your thumbnail? _____

Activity Sheet 3

Classifying Rocks

Draw a picture of a different rock in each box.

Write a description below each picture.

Activity Sheet 4

Looking at Earthworms

Draw a picture of your earthworm in the box.

What does your worm look and feel like?

_____

_____

_____

_____

How does your worm move?

_____

_____

_____

_____

Activity Sheet 5

Looking at Snails

Draw a picture of your snail in the box.

How does your snail eat?

_____

_____

_____

_____

How does your snail move?

_____

_____

_____

_____

Activity Sheet 6

Looking at Fish

Compare two kinds of fish.
How are they the same?
How are they different?

same	**different**
_____	_____
_____	_____
_____	_____
_____	_____
_____	_____
_____	_____
_____	_____
_____	_____
_____	_____

name _____

Fish Outline

Activity Sheet 8

Looking at Leaves

Draw a picture of a different leaf in each box.
Tell how each leaf is different from the others.

_____

_____

_____

_____

_____

_____

name
_____

Looking at Flowers

Draw a picture of a different flower in each box.
Tell how each flower is different from the others.

_____

_____

_____

_____

_____

     LESSON 10

Activity Sheet 10

Color Mixing

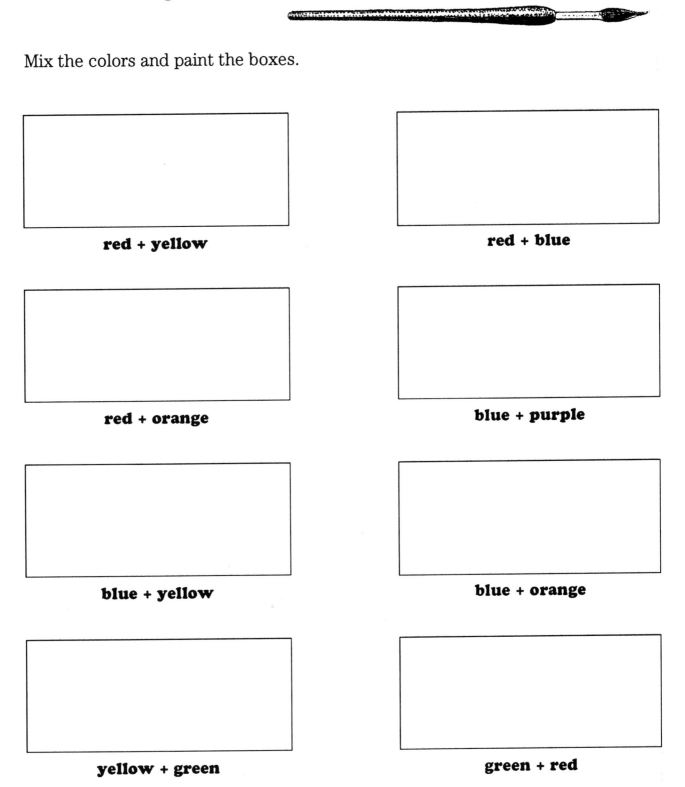

Mix the colors and paint the boxes.

red + yellow

red + blue

red + orange

blue + purple

blue + yellow

blue + orange

yellow + green

green + red

name _____

How Sticky Is It?

Touch each material, and decide whether it is sticky or smooth.
Order the materials from most sticky to most smooth.
List your materials in order here:

most sticky   **1.** _____

              2. _____

              3. _____

              4. _____

              5. _____

              6. _____

              7. _____

              8. _____

              9. _____

most smooth   **10.** _____

Activity Sheet 12

Looking at Baker's Clay

Look at the raw clay.
What does it look and feel like?

_____

_____

_____

_____

_____

Look at the baked clay.
What does it look and feel like?

_____

_____

_____

_____

name _____

How Does It Change?

Draw pictures to show how different foods look
before and after they have been cooked.

before   **after**

© Addison-Wesley Publishing Company

Activity Sheet 14

What's in the Trash?

Draw pictures of things that are thrown away in your home.

name

Moth Outlines

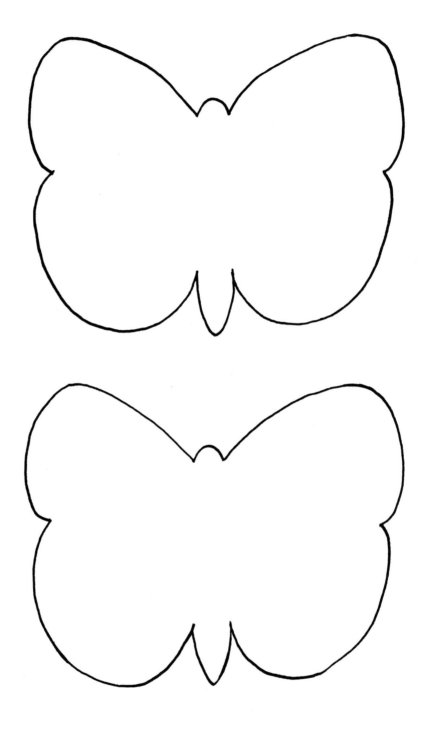

Activity Sheet 16

Classifying Seeds

Seeds that *float* through the air

Seeds that *fall* to the ground

Seeds that *stick* to things

Activity Sheet 17

Energy in My Home

Draw pictures of things that use energy in your home.
Draw one picture in each box.

Activity Sheet 18

Lights in My Home

Draw pictures of different lights in your home.
Draw one picture in each box.

Activity Sheet 19

Color Page

			Key Color			

Activity Sheet 20

Looking at Shadows

dark shadows	light shadows	no shadows

Activity Sheet 21

Butterfly Outline

Activity Sheet 22

Things That Melt

What things in your home will melt when heated?

Draw one picture in each box.

Activity Sheet 23

Classifying Magnetic Objects

Test each object with a magnet.
If it sticks to the magnet, place the object under *magnetic*.
If it does not stick, place the object under *nonmagnetic*.

magnetic   **nonmagnetic**

Appendix

Creativity Without Chaos: Management Tips

Many teachers are concerned about the management of materials and supplies during art and science lessons. Occasionally, such concerns actually prevent teachers from devoting as much time to art and science as they would like.

The key to successful, smoothly flowing lessons is good organization. With planning and preparation, you easily can manage materials and orchestrate efficient cleanup after every art and science lesson.

The following tips come from teachers who have used *The Art and Science Connection* lessons successfully in their classrooms.

How to Stay Organized

- Be sure to read each lesson all the way through before you begin.

- Give yourself time to collect all the materials you need before beginning a lesson. Many items can be brought in by students.

- Have students write their names on the back of their work at the beginning of each lesson.

- Organize students into small groups, and appoint monitors to distribute supplies before the lesson starts. Only the monitors should be allowed to leave their desks during the lesson.

- If possible, recruit one or two upper-grade students to help with distributing materials and cleaning up.

Effective Cleanup Procedures

- Before beginning any lesson, make sure that students understand cleanup procedures and know where to put finished work.

- Cover desks and tables with newspaper. Students can fold odds and ends into the newspaper at cleanup time.

- Collect brushes, pencils, or other implements as a first step in cleaning up. (This stops the art activity.) One monitor can wash brushes later and stand them on their handles in a can to dry.

- Use large brown paper bags from the grocery store as trash cans for each group of students. During cleanup time, monitors can empty the bags into the regular classroom trash can, fold the bags flat, and set them aside for the next art lesson.

- Avoid sink congestion with this handy alternative: provide each student with one wet paper towel and one dry paper towel . These can be distributed loose or in a shallow tub. Have students wipe their hands with the wet towels and dry them with the dry towels, thus avoiding the sink altogether.

Sample Letters to Parent or Guardian

Dear Parent or Guardian:

Our class soon will begin a series of lessons that integrate art and science. Your child will be conducting hands-on science experiments and creating art projects using different media, such as drawing, painting, and sculpture. We need many things for these experiments and projects, so we are asking for your help. If you have any of the following items, please send them to school with your child. All items should be clean and dry.

- small glass jars with lids, such as baby food jars

- drinking straws

- plastic containers with lids, such as margarine tubs

- plastic foam trays

- aluminum pie tins

- newspapers

- coffee can lids

Sincerely,

• •

Dear Parent or Guardian:

Our class soon will begin a lesson on recycling. As part of the lesson, students will use throwaway items to create bas-relief sculptures. We will need a variety of items for this project, so we are asking for your help. If you have any of the following, please send them to school with your child. All items should be clean and dry.

- crushed aluminum cans

- jar lids

- screws, nuts, bolts, wire scraps

- scraps of aluminum foil

- plastic foam trays and cups

- drinking straws

- empty milk and juice cartons

- bits of cardboard

- other safe, nonbreakable throwaway items

Sincerely,

Tips for Working with Art Materials

Working with Tempera

- When mixing powdered tempera, add several drops of dishwashing soap to the paint. This will cause the powdered paint to dissolve more quickly in the water. A few drops of dishwashing soap in liquid tempera will cause the paint to wash off hands more easily.

- Arrange tempera paints in low containers such as cut-off milk cartons or margarine tubs with plastic lids. Arrange containers in shoe boxes for easy storage.

- Collect a variety of plastic containers to use for water. Containers of different sizes can be stored inside each other.

- Individual palettes for color mixing can be made of coffee can or margarine lids, plastic foam trays, and so on.

- When mixing colors, show students how to rinse their brushes and dry them on paper towels so as not to muddy the paints.

Working with Clay

- Use one 25-lb sack of moist clay per class. Check the clay before the lesson to be sure it is still moist.

- Use individual oilcloth place mats to cover desks. If oilcloth is not available, have students use masking tape to fasten fabric-backed wallpaper samples, heavy-duty aluminum sheets, or large flattened paper bags to their work surfaces.

- Use a length of wire for cutting the clay.

- Use plastic bags and rubber bands to store unused clay.

- Provide each group of students with a tub or bucket to wash their hands, and a dry paper towel for each student.

Working with Paste

- Distribute paste on a small scrap of paper for each student.

- When demonstrating collage, show students how to spread the paste on the back of the smaller piece of paper and then stick it to the larger piece.

- Provide wet and dry paper towels for cleanup.

Working with Watercolors

- Demonstrate how to rinse the brush thoroughly with water when mixing colors, so as to avoid muddying colors.

- Show students how to lightly dip the end of a facial tissue onto a wet watercolor pan to remove any muddy color.

- When using crayon-resist techniques, note that some colors resist wax better than others. Different colors are made with different pigments. For instance, browns are heavier than other pigments and tend to lie on the crayon rather than resist it.

- Old, dried-out watercolor pans should be discarded. After several years, the binding agent in the pigments deteriorates, and colors lose their luster.

Working with Chalk

- Reduce the amount of chalk dust produced when students use chalk. Before the activity, soak chalk pieces in water for one or two minutes, and then lay them on newspaper to dry. Using wet chalk will result in brighter colors and less dust, both in the air and on clothing.

- Another way to reduce chalk dust is to have students dip their chalk into liquid starch before applying the chalk to paper. The starch will spread the chalk color over the paper without raising dust. The same technique can be used with white liquid tempera paint on a colored construction paper background.

Tips for Working with Science Materials

The investigations in *The Art and Science Connection* make use of easily available supplies. It is often possible to substitute inexpensive materials for much of the science equipment required in standard experiments.

Droppers

- Use a drinking straw as a homemade dropper:
  1. Fold over the top third of the straw, and pinch the double portion of the straw (not the fold).
  2. Squeeze the straw as you dip it into the water.
  3. Stop squeezing, then lift the straw out of the water.
  4. Squeeze a little bit at a time to make drops come out.

Jars and Other Containers

- For storage, use jam, pickle, peanut butter, and baby food jars, and other types of jars that have tight-fitting lids.
- Use plastic cups of varying sizes to hold liquids during experiments. These can be rinsed thoroughly and used again.
- Use shoe boxes to organize science materials.

Trays

- A plastic foam tray makes an excellent surface on which to examine a snail or collection of pebbles.
- Aluminum pie tins are useful as waterproof trays when students are examining liquids or damp specimens.

Safety Precautions

The lessons in *The Art and Science Connection* generally make use of safe, nontoxic materials. Where more hazardous materials and procedures are called for, safety precautions are carefully outlined within the lesson.

Note: At the beginning of the school year, check with parents or guardians to see if any students have asthma or are allergic to any substances that might be used in a lesson.

The following points apply particularly to the activities contained in the book and are worth noting.

Art Materials: Safety Tips

- Use white glue or paste instead of resin-based glues and rubber cement.

- Use acrylic paints rather than enamel or oil paints.

- Use water-based printing inks rather than oil- or solvent-based inks.

- Use water-based felt markers rather than solvent-based markers.

- Have students wash their hands thoroughly with soap and water after art activities.

Science Materials: Safety Tips

- In handling flowers, take care that pollen is not excessively distributed through the classroom. Some students may be allergic to pollen.

- Only adults should use hot plates or irons during experiments requiring heat, while students observe.

- Caution students against placing any substance or piece of equipment in their mouths.

- Have students wash their hands thoroughly with soap and water after touching animals.

Additional Resources

The Visual Arts

Alexander, Kay. *Learning to Look and Create: The Spectra Program.* Palo Alto, Calif.: Dale Seymour, 1987.

Cohen, Elaine P., and Ruth S. Gainer. *Art: Another Language for Learning.* New York: Schocken Books, 1984.

Edwards, Betty. *Drawing on the Artist Within.* New York: Simon & Schuster, 1986.

Keightley, Moy. *Investigating Art: A Practical Guide for Young People.* Chicago: Facts on File, n.d.

Qualley, Charles. *Safety in the Artroom.* Worcester, Mass.: Davis Publications, 1986.

Rodgriguez, Susan. *The Special Artist's Handbook.* Palo Alto, Calif.: Dale Seymour, 1984.

Uhlin, Donald H., and Edith De Chaira. *Art for Exceptional Children.* (Third edition). Dubuque, Iowa: William C. Brown, 1984.

Wilson, Brent, et al. *Teaching Drawing from Art.* Worcester, Mass.: Davis Publications, 1987.

Science

Allison, Linda, and David Katz. *Gee Wiz! How to Mix Art and Science or the Art of Thinking Scientifically.* Boston: Little, Brown, 1983.

Burke, James. *Connections.* Boston: Little, Brown, 1980.

Gross, Phyllis, and Esther P. Railton. *Teaching Science in an Outdoor Environment.* Berkeley, Calif.: University of California Press, 1972.

Hammerman, Donald R., and William M. Hammerman. *Teaching in the Outdoors.* Minneapolis: Burgess, 1973.

Kramer, David C. *Animals in the Classroom.* Menlo Park, Calif.: Addison-Wesley, 1989.

Lingelbach, Jenepher, ed. *Hands-On Nature: Information and Activities for Exploring the Environment with Children.* Woodstock, Vt.: Vermont Institute of Natural Science, 1987.

Lowery, Lawrence F. *The Everyday Science Sourcebook.* Palo Alto, Calif.: Dale Seymour, 1985.

Nickelsburg, Janet. *Nature Activities for Early Childhood.* Menlo Park, Calif.: Addison-Wesley, 1976.

Ostlund, Karen. *Science Process Skills, Assessing Hands-On Student Performance.* Menlo Park, Calif.: Addison-Wesley, 1992.

Science for All Americans. Washington, D.C.: American Association for the Advancement of Science, 1989.

Sisson, Edith A. *Nature with Children of All Ages.* New York: Prentice-Hall, 1982.

Stein, Sara. *The Science Book.* New York: Workman, 1979.

Strongin, Herb. *Science on a Shoestring.* Menlo Park, Calif.: Addison-Wesley, 1991.

Glossary

acceleration The rate of change of velocity for a moving body. The acceleration may be either a change in direction or a change in speed, or both.

adaptation The modification of an organism or its parts that fits it better for the conditions of its environment.

adhesion The molecular attraction between molecules of different kinds.

atom The smallest particle of an element that can exist either alone or in combination.

baker's clay A dough made of flour, salt, and water that is used for modeling plaques and small sculptures.

balance The arrangement of all parts of an artwork to create a sense of equilibrium.

bas-relief Sculpture in which the forms project only slightly from the surface.

camouflage Protective coloration that disguises an organism, allowing it to hide from its enemies.

capillarity The rising or sinking of a liquid into a small vertical space due to strong adhesion between the materials and surface tension of the liquid.

cohesion The molecular attraction of like molecules for each other.

collage Artwork created by gluing bits of paper, fabric, scraps, photographs, or other materials to a flat surface.

contrast The use of opposites in close proximity, such as light and dark, rough and smooth, and so on.

crayon-resist An art technique in which crayon is applied to paper and then covered with paint. Since wax repels water, the paint will not cover the crayoned part.

current The part of a fluid body moving continuously in a certain direction.

energy In science, the capacity to do work, or to make things move or grow. In the visual arts, energy is vitality of expression.

epidermis The skin, or thin surface layer of primary tissue in higher plants.

evaporation The process by which a substance changes from a liquid to a gas.

force A push or a pull.

gravity The gravitational attraction of the earth's mass for bodies at or near its surface.

heat Thermal energy; the random energy of motion of the molecules of matter.

intensity The brightness or dullness of a color.

interaction A mutual or reciprocal action or influence.

liquid A substance that flows; the fluid state of matter where the molecules or atoms are in contact, but where the bonding forces are too weak to hold them still with respect to one another.

magnetic force A repulsive or attractive force between the poles of magnets.

mass The quantity of matter in a body.

matter A substance that constitutes the observable universe. The substance of which a physical object is composed.

mixed-media The use of several different materials or techniques in one work of art.

molecule The smallest particle of an element or compound that retains chemical identity with the substance in mass.

monoprint A one-of-a-kind impression of a design or picture created on another surface.

mosaic A pattern or design made by placing many small pieces of rock, tile, glass, or other items together.

mural A work of art that is applied to a wall surface.

opaque Neither reflecting nor emitting light; not translucent or transparent.

plaque A flat thin piece (as of metal or clay) used for decoration.

plaster of Paris A white powdery substance used for casts and molds in the form of a quick-setting paste with water.

primary colors Red, yellow, and blue; those colors that are the basis for mixing all other colors.

recycle To use again.

repetition An element of design in which the artist uses repeating colors, lines, shapes, or patterns.

secondary colors Orange, green, and purple; those colors that are made by mixing pairs of primary colors.

solid A substance that keeps its shape when it is left alone; any material whose atoms are bonded in place with respect to their nearby neighbors, giving the matter shape and strength.

structure In science, the arrangement of particles or parts in a substance or body. In the visual arts, a design or organization of independent parts to form a coordinated whole.

symmetry An element of design in which a sense of balance is achieved by the use of identical or similar colors, lines, shapes, or designs on either side of the center.

temperature The measure of thermal energy of a substance.

texture The appearance and feel of a surface: rough, smooth, bumpy, and so on.

translucent Partly transparent; admitting some light.

transparent Clear; transmitting light so that objects beyond are completely visible.

value The lightness or darkness of colors.

variation on a theme Within a work of art, a change in form, shape, detail, or appearance that makes an object different from similar objects.

Table of Visual-Arts Media Skills

Media Skills	Lessons
Drawing	
▪ Charcoal	22
▪ Crayon	10, 17, 21, 22, 26
▪ Chalk	23
▪ Ink	10, 17
Painting	
▪ Tempera	2, 15, 21, 28, 29
▪ Watercolor	12
▪ Sand	4
Sculpture	
▪ Clay	30
▪ Constructions in Space	8, 20
▪ Baker's Clay	14
▪ Bas-Relief	16, 21
Printmaking	
▪ Vegetable Prints	6, 9
▪ Stamp Prints	11
▪ Monoprints	13
Collage	
▪ Paper	18, 19, 24
▪ Mosaics	5
▪ Murals	21
Graphic Arts	
▪ Posters	17
Mixed Media	3, 7, 21, 27

Table of Science Topics

Topics	Lessons
Life Science	
▪ Plants	9, 10, 20
▪ Animals	6, 7, 8, 18, 19
▪ Ecosystems	21
Earth Science	
▪ Geology	4, 5
▪ Natural Resources	16, 17
▪ Oceanography	29
Physical Science	
▪ Matter	1, 2, 3, 12, 13, 28
▪ Chemistry	14
▪ Mechanics	15
▪ Heat	14, 22, 27, 28, 29
▪ Light	11, 22, 23, 24, 25, 26
▪ Magnetism	22, 30